Hello Couture: Fetish Garden

Channah Morozyukova

FARI PUBLISHING
LONDON | NEW YORK

FARI PUBLISHING

Published by Fari Publishing

Printed in the United States of America.
Published simultaneously in United Kingdom, and Canada.

Library of Congress Control Number: 2012954354

ISBN 978-0-615-73274-9

FIRST EDITION

Typography: Cochin, Gothic

PUBLISHER'S NOTE

The advice contained herein is for informational purposes only.
This book is not a substitute for psychological treatment, or for
medical care by a physician. The author and the publisher disclaim
any and all liability for any consequences, damages, and
outcomes (including property damage, physical injury, or death)
that may occur as resulting from the use of the information
contained in this book.

Thematic Photography
Photography: Channah Vladimirovna Morozyuk
Photography: Jeff Carrillo. Front Cover, & Page 27, 253.
Hair & Makeup: Lina Hang. Front Cover, & Page 27, 253 -
Channah Vladimirovna Morozyuk for remaining pages.

For More Information Visit:
WWW.FARIPUBLISHING.COM

YOU HAD ME @ HELLO.

Dedication
To my mentor Dr. Lucy Tama Sogoian, i am grateful for the guidance, massive support, and precious times our families shared together, love you infinte.
i write this book, a love letter for all of you that embark onto this mindful journey of enlightenment.
The path of love and self-love.

M A N I F E S T self+LOVE. self+compAssion.

Acknowledgments
I thank G_d for all his blessings, for His Angels and Spirit Guides, I thank my beloved ancestors whom are with me, and providing guidance, love and eternal Love. My Father, Sheldon for teaching me steadfast integrity, our family's

ancestral legacy throughout my life and more. My Mother P.R. MFA for cultivating me as an old soul, Priestess, a spiritual being. introducing me to our family's spiritual legacy at the age of four and harnessing the spirit within. i love you both and I love you all.

as an ancestral beacon my mission is to spread LOVE. Self+LOVE. I am, a practicing third Generation Shaman.

About the Author

Spirituality is earned. As an initiated Oshun Priestess (Goddess/Deity of Love, sexuality, pleasure, fertility, prosperity, beauty and Love) and Third Generation Shaman, I've devoted my life to study and practice in becoming a leader of self+LOVE and beauty, a Shaman for people all over the world, to awaken your inner Goddess within. I have learned, studied world religions and spirituality and initiated in what is known as the "religion" a crowned Saint. Also i've spent twelve months of my life in a monastery swathed entirely in white abstinence from sex. i've done more than a few HARD-CORE initiations. I come from a long lineage of spiritual practitioners. My Mother is an initiated Oya Priestess, and taught me ancient voodoo recipes of healing, botany and more! On my maternal side of the family i also come from a long lineage of Voodou and my Great-Great Grandmother a High Priestess worked with Voodoo Queen Marie Laveau.
The Paternal side of me is Shamanism, i am great - great granddaughter of the Legendary Choctaw Chief Greenwood McCurtain. i am, Shaman(s) gain power through ancestor spiritual mounting, sacred ceremonies and spiritual inheritance, i have received these blessings from my shamanic path from hundreds of years and i am spiritual heir of that Legacy, i am a modern day Shaman from indigenious teachings.
i have created biodynamic cosmetics as a catalyst to spread self+Love. I make makeup to spread the vibration Of love, as a mantra. The cosmetics are nourishment for the body and soul, to bring out your authentic glow, and tap into you're self-love, inner Love Goddess. i am the first to create LOVE POTION makeup and also a formula of cosmetics that are infused with white quartz, and Rose Quartz powder into mineral makeup, as i was channeled to do so and with meta+physical properties! The mission is to infuse more self+Love into the world

It's made in small-batches by ancient native and shamanic methods, in accordance to moon cycles, surrounded by crystals for beauty and love energy. 99% of Lubov Cosmetics are crafted with Sacred adornment, scented with blessed essential oils and infused with Love energy! (love & light)
Lubov Cosmetics is my other vessel, a beacon to spread beauty, self-love, self+compassion, and for beings to

regain youthfulness, and good vibes. I want beings to realize that this life is to be present, mindful and enjoy your life! Life is what you Create.
Make this life your own Garden of Eden..... the tools, botanical's, elements are here for you to create and be surrounded by beauty and Love.

hello. welcome to the Fetish Garden, get ready to amplify, self!

This book itself is an Art Installation, an inspiring self-help guide. Journey.
In this badass self-help how-to-guide. With, Indigenous teachings translated into a contemporary Art Installation via. Coffee table book for spiritual beings -wanting to tap into their inner feminine Love Goddess.
Hello Couture, Fetish Garden is an inspiring radical interactive self-help guide.. Hello Couture: Fetish Garden, is a daily handbook ... guide giving you the tools to awaken the awesome power within, self-love fetishism; turning it into a daily habit, and as we take this journey you will find mindful exercises, using clever word play "contemporary text art" forcing positive affirmations into the sub-conscious.
i cut out all the B.S. with CliffsNotes of self empowerment and aura cleansing recipes, to unf*ck yourself.
Say hello, F*ck that negativity shit. Transform your energy to self-love.

Hello, i am Priestess. Shaman Channah Lubov Great -Great Granddaughter of the Legendary Choctaw Chief Greenwood McCurtain, McCurtain County, Oklahoma named in honor of the McCurtain Dynasty, my family. i'm Spiritual heir, Shaman on Father's side. 3rd Generation Shaman / Priestess on Mother's side, i've studied virtually all the world's major spiritual paths personally trained by my Spritual family since the age of four, later to be initiated into what is know as the Religion, belonging to one of the oldest respected houses in the community, It's not something that you choose, you are chosen by your Ancestors and Spirit Guides regardless of what you actually want, yet later you gracefully, humbly, wholehearted embrace.
This book is a tool for your RADICAL TRANSFORMATION of self-Love and spread the love into the UniverSe. Let us be supportive of one another. i want to spread my love for all that seek their authentic self. My intent is for you to embrace, reclaim and awaken your self-love, it's a EUPHOriC feeling, you shall see things differently as YOU ARE AWAKE(N). Rid your concsiousness of judgement and criticism. Self-love is about letting yourself receive all that is good, Love. Love yourself internally, spirit, body and soul the divine you. This is my manifesto, for you.. a garden of Love for YOU to transform and reach your Optimal potential. In this book i'm litterally spraying what i call my Self-Love, Love Spray on you..... for you to find self+compassion, love. your soulmate within.
Believe in the love tribe, it's pride and celebration of self+love, for all. i have tuned into the energy of the universe, the need for this Love book is a cataylist, a vessal for people to cut chaoS to find self. i find self-help books using incomprehensible words, intimidating and hard to learn.. So i made thiS book fun!
Also use this visually, as a kitsch "mindfulness" flash (card) book for another level....
Spirituality and inner growth is for everyone and all ages that is why i have written the text in basic plain english, to make this journey a practical guide and EASY TO FOLLOW steps with subliminal stimuli illusion.
This book is for all. Let us all belong to the same tribe that is, love for all humankind, the love tribe.
The Calling: The relationship between things, information and purpose.
my paths that brought me to this calling, my Art spreads the message, of Love and circulating the energy of love via HELLO COUTURE and LUBOV COSMETICS is made from raw love energy to spread more Love and Good Vibes into the Universe! Some insights, at a young age I was introduced to spirituality from both sides of my family. as a teenager I was an extra in a cult film, Mtv muSic video vixen, almost a thespian in high school and modeling.... always seeking my truth. I was introduced to beauty, art, fashion and spirituality by both of my parents. Love 'urself unapologetically, no regrets is how you grow and learn in life is through experienIce. Learn to listen. Grow. be non-judgemental. Live your best life. Spirituality, being a Shaman in the beginning of life there are crossroads, and different lives(paths), a nomad, all to bring you to have empathy, unconditional love for life, unconditional love for people. the Shaman's calling, takes you on different paths (Dimensions) in life, [for me these hard lessons came at an early age, so now/the present the future my life is tranquil, lavish, and has wellbeing, for me to connect and spread the teachings of self+Love. I want you to have a higher understanding and expand the consciousness. Be present. mindfulness , for fulfillment. Self+Care a mindful Lifestyle.
Be your best soulmate, but first you must find self+worth, self+love and wellbeing.

i searched for my soulmate.... to find i am. Have you found your soulmate? are you preSent?

Because of my upbringing, i've always been motivated from beauty, fashion, Art and Spirituality as a daily routine. Learned to use crystals daily, they were my breakfast of champions.

So how did I get to this point of the journey? to make a long story short....

Living many lives in such a short period of time that i wanted to find my authentic self. Interned at a Beverly Hill's Talent Agency while a freshman in college, thereafter worked for a Beverly Hill's Talent Management company. Whilst also moonlighting as a model and music video vixen which the later is still playing and rocking on MTV Germany and Latin America.

A few years later even though modeling is enjoying and so on... i wanted to return to fashion, my first love, also my grandmother was a seamstress and taught me how to sew as a young girl, the earlyist item remembered sewing was a red heart shaped pillow with embellished lace, actually when you think about it my destiny was already set in stone. From this to fashion design school in Downtown Los Angeles. After graduation wanting to achieve more knowledge and hardcore training I worked in L..A.'s authentic fashion sewing factories that were sweatshops, my work aesthetic is to start from the bottom and work your way up, no nepotism, it builds character and to be honest people that work in sweatshops are actually sewing and pattern Guru's and I have the upmost respect for them they deserve more acclaim! What came next, when becoming of age I went through my Priesthood, and Shamanic studies officially making a full circle into my life, at this point I would go into full detail yet this part of my life is quite lengthy, and is a book in itself. In short, Initiation is actually as you might think, prayers, obedience, tradition, abstinence of various food, no alcoholic beverages, no makeup, I wasn't allowed to look in the mirror, no Masturbation no sex of any kind for at least a year! Many rules, secrecy to become a priestess and a shaven head, when at the time it wasn't cool whilst wearing special guru attire.... and more abstinence. I actually slept on a concrete floor for a whole year as well as eating without fork, nor knife on a straw mat placed upon the floor. An elder gives you a detailed map of basically your entire life from rules of do's and dont's, actually it's a look into your future, that is why it's called a life reading, it's truly intense! Generally it takes at least all day and taken quite seriously as those in the religion have learned it's to be respected as your receiving this information via ancestors and spirits speaking directly to you during this reading that's absolutely mind blowing and 100% destiny!

Because of my past experiences a spiritual awakening happened, at a crossroads with my career and coming from a spiritual artistic family, the need to take a sabbatical, a spiritual journey to Live Life on the road and find my passion, my true authentic purpose, Shamanic/Priestess.

Shortly after that time I caught and was hospitalized with the Swine Flu, it was a miracle I was cured, what really comes to mind is the cliche is to really live life but with a purpose, do what makes you happy and it's a simple message but spread love, help people. and how to fuse everything into one Love child - love, art, makeup, spirituality and beauty, while spreading the word of love and beauty, everyone has their own beauty. Bring people to unite.

And so it began...destination shall find you

And so it began...destination shall find YOU!

I wasn't living my truth, so while on the road one night I had a spiritual visit on the road, in the southwest I wasn't surprised as traveling through the empty lonesome opened aired mystic southwest hwys at night there as a Shaman one sees and hear's alot of trippy things during a.m. hours on during after hours with the bright stars shining brightly they being the light and under hallowed beaming moonlight, ethereal voices (by the way shamanic powers are inherited) told me to spread love, i am a vessal of love. They told me my purpose... and do what I love..... spread love through my beauty products with sacred adornment, and teach everyone that will listen that everyone has their own beauty, inside and out, beauty is love. By spreading more love... when people are happy and have self-love they can love, be love... love creates positive energy vibrations and makes the world the universe better as they say, "every bit helps, for us to unite in unity for love and light in this world." Good vibrations create more positive vibes and goodness in the universe. My journey is to help people fall in love with themselves to feel fulfilled so they no longer thirst and feed on the negativity that brings self-loathing. Love is love. Love is life....

My Spirit Guide, my archetype Ochun, Aphrodite/Venus the Goddess of Love, sexuality, fertility, money and beauty, she is the orisha of sweetness everything that makes life worth living. The femme fetale of the orishas and once saved the world. The Goddess and other paths of love goddesses has chosen me to spread the message of love and self-love, and beauty (as we all have our own beauty, do not settle for the cookie-cutter of what society defines as beauty. We are all beautiful in our own way) I am one of her (a) vessel(s) to spread hope, love, happiness and beauty. Ochun is the savior, nurturer of humanity! My life's journey I have claimed....awaken and risen within me, body, spirit, soul, mentally and literally accepted who I am on my own freewill, not because the spirituality has been in my family or expected of me or of the legacy, i have fully and lovingly embraced that I am, a Shaman, a Priestess to help people from all walks of life.

Now I have this level of determination – I'm on a mission of Love. We make love complicated and over think it, yet honestly, with the proper tools i'm here to teach you to love yourself.. it isn't easy but it is simple.

Beauty, love, and Self-Love Ritual
Start your day with love.....Morning Mirror Mantra, perfect for manifesting love and self-love. Meditate with your crystal(s), for beauty and healing use Rose quartz the stone of universal love. This quartz has metaphysial properties, inspires unconditional love, the love of beauty, and self-love. Also used to attract love, this is the ultimate stone for love (carry this stone with you and also keep in bedroom for self love healing and attracting love).
Stare into the mirror. Spray your favorite perfume or room diffuser of your favorite sent. Set your intentions. Say out loud this mantra with intent, I Love myself & I and I Love you, or use your own words that you want to manifest for beauty, and or love with intentions... now apply your makeup. This is a time set aside for you to appreciate yourself fall in love with yourself and create your own magic.
Once upon a time they considered makeup witchcraft, and women would use cosmetics as sorcery as a way to get married... a love spell.
Note, the word glamour originally defined as an illusion, magic charm spell.

Contents:

Do you like to watch? voyeuristic?
Most of us do like to watch....

this is an interactive. visual. playful. made easy self-help guide.
Hello loves, I created this journey for the new times the age of enlightenment.... we live in an era whereas media reports most people have a short attention span, shorter than a Goldfish, even social media is a aware that our attention span is getting shorter. For example a large social media platform gives a whole whopping 60 SEcONDS for video uploading viewing. Neuropsychologial studies are not corroborated, yet an article in Psychology Today suggests it's due to all the distractions from social media and the internet. I've researched and through medative channeling I was guided the proper tools to awaken the easily distracted YOU, to awaken your human consciousness for healing to bring forth YOUR self-love.

Let the trip begin. Sit back, relax and discover YOU...
Mindfulness. I want you to notice your surroundings, not just the obvious.
Step outside your comfort zone-challenge yourself to follow through daily, with a self-love act. Instinctively use your healing energy within to look at yourself with love and watch yourself telling "you" something lovingly about YOUR "Self" Set a reminder to follow through daily, now as you watch yourself.... analyze the way you speak to yourself and others.
Do you want to sound seductive, monotone or with warmth? find your authentic self the truth is within you, when you find your voice use these words as your own personal affirmation.

Are you aware... Be Present.
The physical body has a bio-magnetiC field of energy when you project a happy positive vibe you attract the same energy.... that is why it's important to empower your inner voice and have a vibe of happiness...love. Remember you are magnetic, whatever your vibe is at that time that is what you shall attract. Be patient, just like when you first date someone you like... love takes time. By way of example consider when you plant a garden you have to nourish, water, feed, cultivate and when you treat it with love it loves you in return with blooms.. bloom forever.
Stalking Nature with Love and Light.
I want you to open yourself to the beauty, notice the vastly beautiful and lovely surroundings in our environment. When you travel notice all and delight in the undiscovered and then rediscover with virginal visionary and our five senses. Our environment is an epic journey to be discovered in a fresh viewpoint. Be inspired, be fresh always in your way of thinking.. this wondrous atmosphere that surrounds us daily take nothing for granted yet take advantage of the love and light that is upon us. Let us exile ourselves from downers and negativity. Awaken. Be present. I want you to fall in love with YOU.

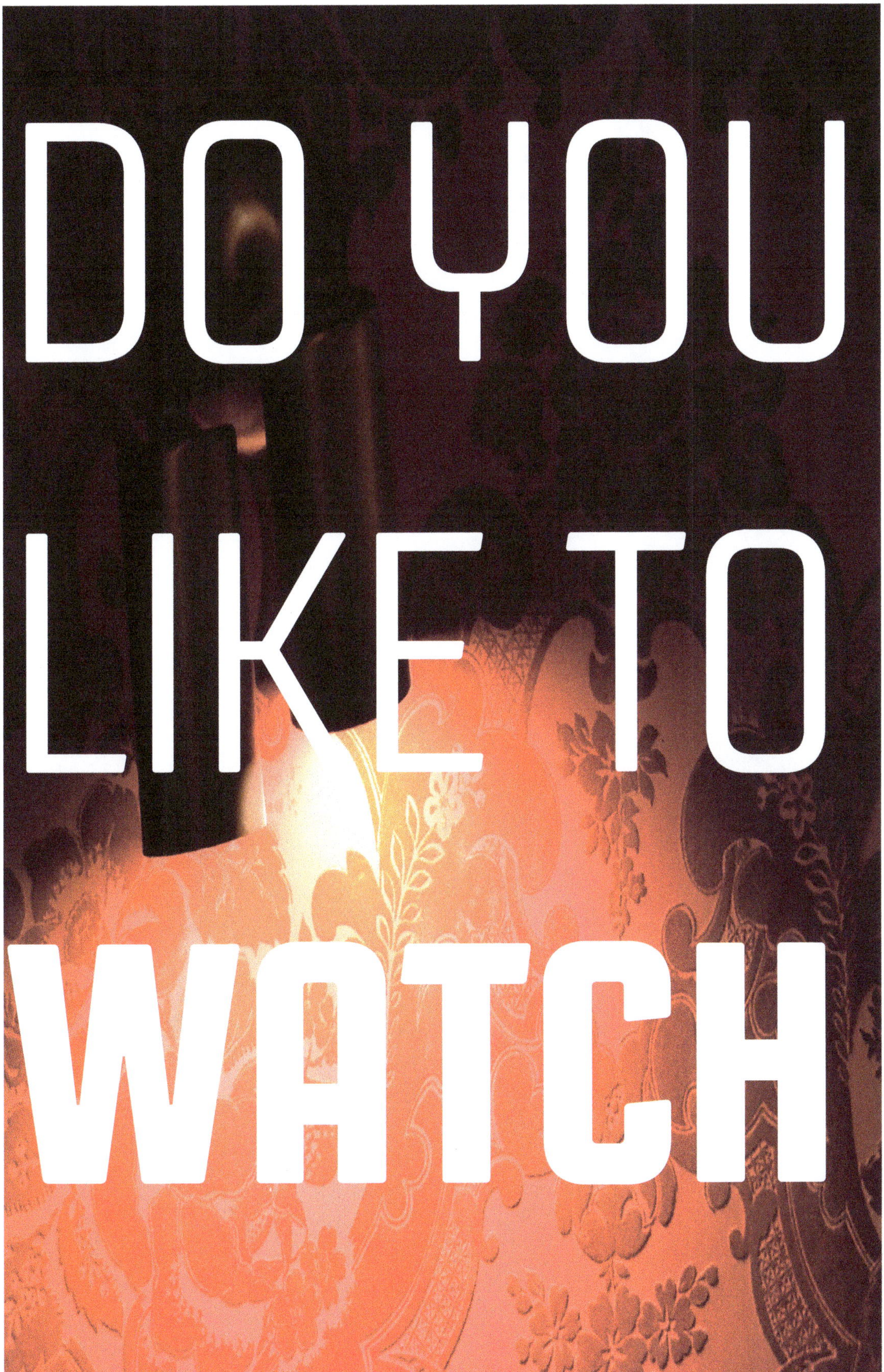
DO YOU
LIKE TO
WATCH

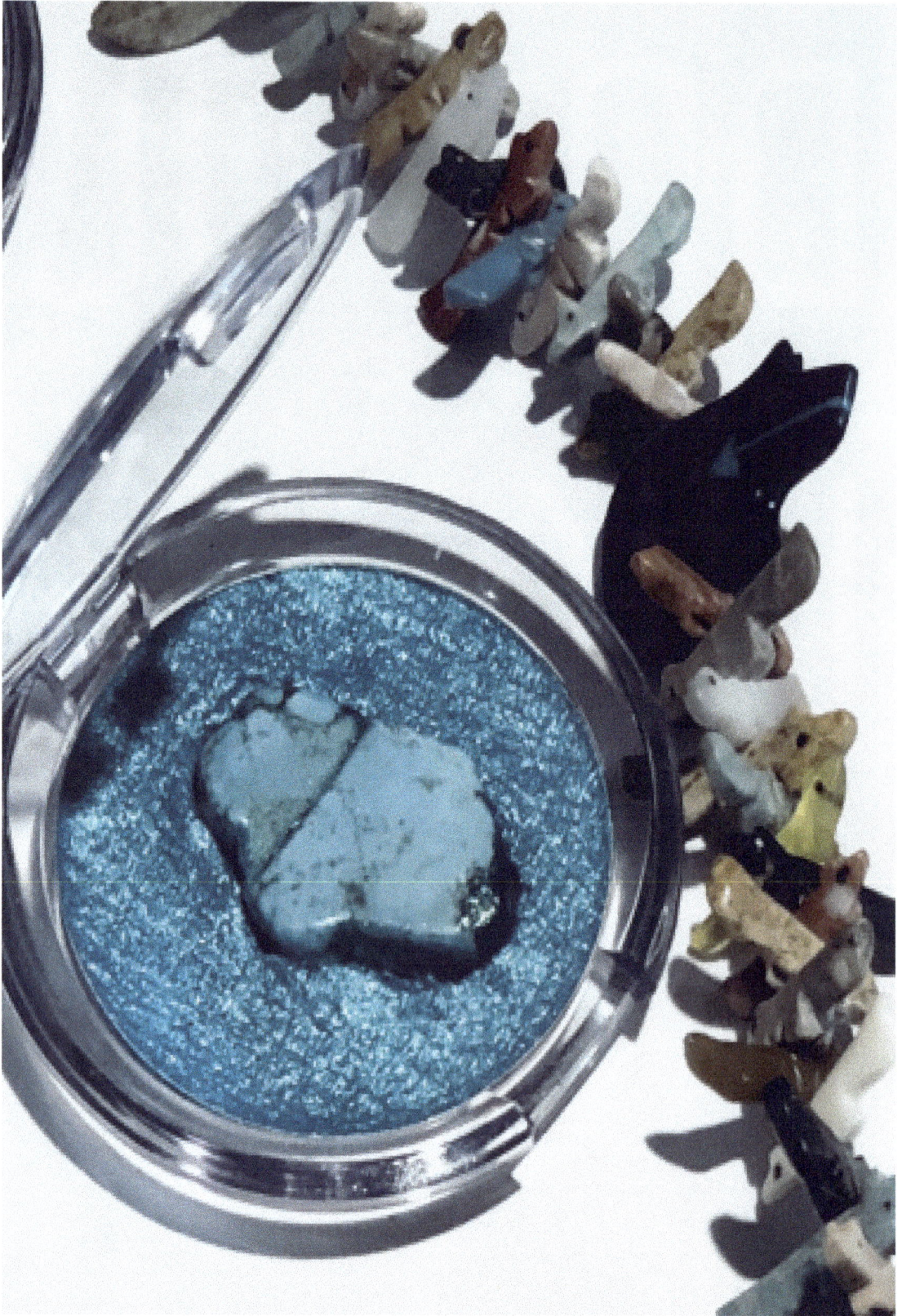

BE awestruck at the Plethora of Love when you share Love.

Take a trip to self+discovery unapologetic mind-fuck, for positive change.
Self-love is a state of mind. I want you to begin by, throwing away mental judgement of others and yourself. Let all negative clutter slide off of you like okra juice. Forgive and forget, make this one of your mantras as the universe shall shield you when you let go of negativity, whenever someone tries to get a reaction do not feed negativity have control over your emotions, anger is the ego's lack of self+confidence. Be the person of beauty and sweetness. Arouse positive energy by being proactive and love someone when they are not being their best. Accept love unconditionally and be love. Once you practice loving yourself and others even the simple things in life you will have fulfillment and satisfaction, giving always feels rewarding. Positive actions yield less negativity and chaos in your life.

IN THE MOOD. conscious actions.
Getting started, make it a good-habit to be ever-growing positive energy.
Find a space where you are most comfortable. Indulge. Light incense your favorite candle(s) do nothing just go into yourself. Identify. Do this meditation daily, find what time best suits your inner being as repetition reinforces good habits.
note: i find that one's favorite scent in a candle, really helps to put you...in the mood.

HOMEWORK
In this book you will find journal pages to write personal notes (for self-discovery), I want you to carefully document what stimulates your five senses: visual, auditory, taste, feel, sensory, engage in your senses making you feel totally uninhibited. Navigate your feelings on the journal pages. Now lets focus our eyesight and gaze upon textured layers of visionary tales, provoking emotions of what we are seeing. Look within ourselves, we all have certain images and fetishes that can awaken a hunger making us starved for a visionary tale. We are voyeurs from organic nature.

a coffee table book is an oversized, picturesque book usually used for an artistic display on a table intended for use
in an area that entertains guests and provokes inspired conversation. you will learn Love tribe to be mindful and use
this as a coffee table book, a beautiful consistent daily reminder to stimulate your mind, body and spirit. By doing this exercise in rep·e·ti·tion daily you are forming a habit, practicing self+Love.

fet·ish
fetish : an inanimate object worshiped for its magical super natural powers. also ancient beliefs say it is inhabited by a spirit. Each piece is a masterpiece & handmade with meta+physical properties under the moonlight.

What turns us on? Do we like to watch? Actually, our vision is a catalyst of the next step to what we are going to feel or how we are going to react. Looking at visuals is a catalyst to stimulate our minds in being more receptive of a message allowing us to open ourselves up to a positive energy bio-magnetic field, sometimes we can have a total recall to a pleasant memory when we allow ourselves It can be quite detailed; "a warm sunrise basking upon our morning naked skin" to a phallic symbol that makes us breath a little harder, taking us back to a pleasant past memory or a new daydream.

Sometimes what we see causes instant relaxed gratification. Awesome, right? I want this book to take you on an enigmatic satisfying journey. With thoughts of sensuality. You are intelligent and beautiful...Believe in you're self! You are sensual and you are opening yourself, to be present look at your surrounding environment with dilated drunken pupils in love with nature, at home take out something you love that you can see in your environment daily, rather than saving it for the future, the future is today. The world is deliciously wondrous. Whatever road you encounter be present, stop and peel the layers of the beauty that is in front of you, take in the positive beauty.

Let me take you on a ride of gyrating beauty, humor, lust and innocent stimulation. This is a celebration of being comfortable within. Read this book sitting, laying down or upside down in lotus position or 69 but do read uninhibited. Sit back, enjoy, and indulge in the fetish garden....

a place. a journey. of self-discovery & LOVE.

enjoy the ride of life. Life is actually a roller coaster ride, you have your ups and downs. Although it can be easier if you don't sweat the little things, always look at the bright side of life be aware that regardless of any situation their are always solutions. We all make mistakes and when we are evolved we learn to make lemons into lemonade, from sour we make it sweet. Instead of worrying meditate on the universe and or you're guide(s) the question, " what do i need to know?" it will come to you do not stress, the answer will come from within to resolve as your guides and nature will always help you if it's meant to be. Also do not force answers instead, go outdoors, relax enjoy the amazing nature that surrounds us, take deep breaths, until you climax from your surroundings taking the edge off. Negativity and chaos loves to attach to people when they vibrate low. Vibrate high, take yourself out of exile when problems arise, rise your vibration. again go outdoors into the ray of light, if you live near a beach go there and bask in the sun receiving energy and your vitamin D. Learn to enjoy what the universe has created a scenery that is remarkably brilliant in every aspect, nourishing. When you indulge into nature you can find its organically orgasmic. Sit back and enjoy this trip and dig the scenery. whilst you open yourself to the universe the proper option shall BE awestruck at the Plethora of love when you share love.

" BE a Revolution of LOVE. Forgive and forget, make this one of your mantras, and let go of idle gossip. BE awestruck at the Plethora of love when you engage in good vibrations and share love. Be inspiring for yourself and others"

Take a trip to self discovery in the fetish garden that is a Love for all things in beauty. an unapologetic self-love, sensual mind-fuck for positive change.
Self-love is a state of mind. I want you to begin by, throwing away mental judgement of others and yourself. Let all negative clutter slide off of you like okra juice. Forgive and forget, make this one of your mantras as the universe shall shield you when you let go of negativity, whenever someone tries to get
a reaction do not feed negativity have control over your emotions, anger is the ego's lack of self-confidence. Be the person of intelligence, beauty and sweetness. Arouse positive energy by being proactive and love someone when they are not being their best. Accept love unconditionally and be love. Once you practice loving yourself and others even the simple things in life you will have fulfillment and satisfaction, giving always feels rewarding. Positive actions yield less negativity and chaos in your life negativity, whenever someone tries to get a reation do not feed negativity have ontrol over your emotions, anger is the ego's lack of self+confidene. Be the person of beauty and sweetness. Arouse positive energy by being proactive and love someone when they are not being their best. Accept love unconditionally and be love. Once you practice loving yourself and others even the simple things in life you will have fulfillment and satisfaction, giving always feels rewarding. Positive actions yield less negativity and chaos. LOVE-makes-the-world-go-round.

Mindfulness. The final exercise for you in this book is to be present.
LIVE. be aware of all the raw beauty that surrounds you and be sweet and thoughtful to others. LOVE. Remember we are notorious with our actions, stay strong focused in your intent. Whenever your mood needs a positive reminder, let this book guide you and be the uplifting boost when you need it!

Wherever YOU are in life, always remember what's inside of you is intelligent, full of love, pretty fabulous and beautiful. Let this be one of your affirmations and always do something that benefits another., make this a good habit.

Its quite fulfilling when you do a kind act, be creative.

PLAY.

Enter the seductive and mysterious world, of fetish excluding the typical subject of s&m and nudity a fetish can be anything...Literally speaking there is more to explore as a voyeur and or a participant, fetish objects, et cetera. My work explores this philosophy and the phatasmagoric form of the relation between things. I've been told that i'm a relentless traveler, let me share this experience with you. i'm taking you on a mindful journey into a seductive, mysterious and intimate space, a trip of love. I lived life on the road traveling for over two years, photographically capturing and documenting, visionary tales. I taken photos that lifted my eyebrows and peaked my curiosity, wanting to share, whilst making others aware of the extraordinary visionary ongoings. For the most part I didn't take pictures of the obvious and tourist attractions, yet the not obvious. With this in mind i'm bringing you subjects in their raw and natural state. Please enjoy. I hope that these images find you perk, zesty and inspired every day. i want you to see beauty in everything! Fetish are innate part of the human psyche. Find your healthy fetish garden to fulfill YOU.

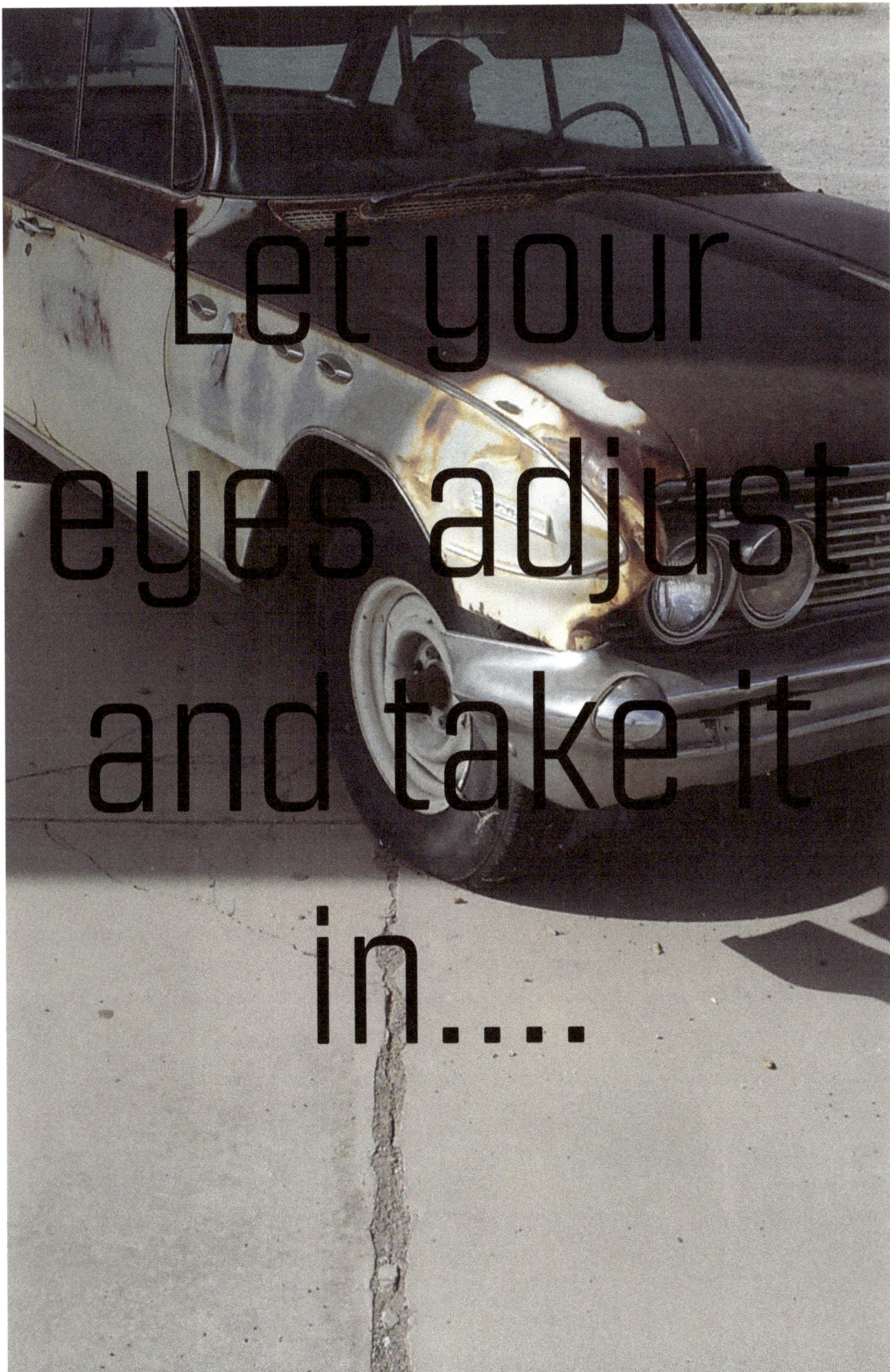

Let your
eyes adjust
and take it
in.....

BE LOVE.

Engage in love. Enrich our society with positive thoughts. The world can be completely beautiful, it's a beautiful thing. - if we look upon one another and not search for our differences and diversity. Let's connect to positive energy!
Are you aware that every action you do is being observed and evaluated to determine how much blessings you are to receive?

Be love. Be inspirational and say hello everyday, with a smile to strangers, spread positive energy into the universe. Celebrate World Hello Day November 21 of every year. Everyday spread acceptance, Peace & Love, communication ....

Be socially conscious....show compassion and value others in high regard. Lets get rid of labels and pre-judgemental stereo-types, prejudices.
Let us break out of the captivity of discrimination from yesteryear. Free your mind by not filing people in categories, stop making people feel asif they are outsiders make a difference in the future showing that as a spirirtual being we have grown and learned from history of past mistakes from the unevolved, and channel the energy of compassion, love for other peoples feelings...humanity.
Let everyone in the New Age movement/Millennials be the change, and stop bullying people because you think they are different, we are all unique and beautiful, we can all learn something from one another to grow and become better people. Let us all say, you can sit with us, and stop alienating people. Spirituality is understanding, unconditional love with no judgement and having empathy for others. No one on this earth is perfect we all have our stories, so let us help one another to vibrate high. Life is a work in progress do something out of your comfort zone, start out simplistic be proactive in making a difference today and everyday. There is a huge awakening taking place we are in a new era, new age. Our awareness of spiritual growth to be better beings and spreading love will bring positive results to humanity, and by working on ourselves we are sharing in this weallth to create compassion for all, the tribe of love.

HAND-sewn.

Immerse yourself in the ultimate experience of a two year voyeuristic journey across the United States Of America from a relentless joyride. I'm delighted to say after twenty-five thousand images derived from this journey here is my sweat, tears and laughter of what was an incredible, emotionally trippy experience that added to my spiritual growth, to share a growing experience with you, the universe is teaching us if we are open to listen that their is always room to grow and learn as long as we live we must be receptive vessals to learn more. When you do something in goodwill from the heart - donot do it in hopes for it to return, do good unto others beause it fulfills you. There are many acts of compassion, love... you can do for humankind, be creative.

Law of Attraction

The photos in this book are only referenced by place, i want you the reader to open yourself (affirmation: I welcome positivity into my life), and have your own visual perception to the images. Let this book be the place for you to create a space of growth within, harness the power of love and discovery think outside of the box, and welcome the self-love lifestyle of.. Hello Couture: fetish garden, a

place of LOVE, self-love, self-Compassion, beauty and enchantment.
I want you to HAND-sew LOVE with one another whilst embracing the great cornucopia of what nature/ethereal landscape has to offer visually and more.
Most importantly "I want you to fall in LOVE" with yourself, Love yourself.
Be open, let this book inspire you... show compassion to yourself and all...

we are more than human beings
we are spiritual beings...

Affirmation tap into the feminine energy

You are a Goddess. You are a Goddess.
You are a Goddess. You are a Goddess.
You are a Goddess. You are a Goddess.
You are a Goddess. You are a Goddess.
You are a Goddess. You are a Goddess.
You are a Goddess. You are a Goddess.
You are a Goddess. You are a Goddess.
You are a Goddess. You are a Goddess.
You are a Goddess. You are a Goddess.
You are a Goddess. You are a Goddess.
You are a Goddess. You are a Goddess.
You are a Goddess. You are a Goddess.
You are a Goddess. You are a Goddess.
You are a Goddess. You are a Goddess.
You are a Goddess. You are a Goddess.

FETISH: ANY OBJECT, AN IDEA, THAT CREATES A HABITUAL EROTIC RESPONSE OR FIXATION.

DO YOU LIKE TO WATCH. Xx
A Documentary photographic tale in chronological order taken
in two years across the United States Of America from a
"mindfulness "
joyride. (of my fetish garden)

Welcome to the fetish garden a place of enchantment, land of
self-love. inner fulfillment and well being through visual tools.
Hello's.. and Love, pass it on..

Chapter 1

Beverly Hills Grass.

JANUARY

LIFE ISN'T COHESIVE, IT'S PRETTY RANDOM
BE SPONTANEOUS." Yet there is no such thing as Coincidence.

Be PRESENT. GROW into BOUNDLESS POWER

Beverly Hills, where the grass is pretty green.
Every month be inspired. Surround yourself in the beauty of the earth. Let's look and watch everything that surrounds us in a positive fulfilling light.
Let's start with Beverly Hills, California. Let us notice something that isn't the obvious.
THIS TOWN HAS A SCENT OF FRESHLY CUT GREEN GRASS?

Be Present:
I have found EVERY TOWN HAS THEIR OWN AU NATURAL PERFUMED NOTE SCENT. unique. Find the magic in your town, allow your life to be blessed, YOU deserve to be fulfilled. Don't wait, to find happiness. where are you now in life? money doesn't buy happiness. Some people think wealth, fame, and power will bring them hapiness, it won't fulfill you if your not happy with yourself. Self+Love is fulfillment. Enjoy your life in the present. Find the goodvibes wherever you live. ...this town. your town, truly has something magical and brilliant about it, even the lush grass here is lined in love and glamorously sprinkled in magic dust, where dreams come true, it's called self+love.
Wherever you are let the grass be greener and inspirational.

Just close your eyes. wet your lips. put on Lubov powdered
crystal infused lipstick, helps to awaken....LOVE.
self+LOVE. self+compssion

feed your inner goddess in love soaked dress...and you'll
find your being kissed by an organic luminous sexy fairytale.
You are blessed with the power to Create your love garden.
You are blessed with the power to manifest a fairytale life.
You are blessed to Create what you desire...
CAPTURE THIS NEW YEAR AND EVERY NEW YEAR IN A LOVE AFFAIR
OF SELF-LOVE. BE PASSIONATE. CELEBRATE LIFE,
LOVE AND LIVE LIFE. YOU HAVE THE POWER TO M A N I F E S T

Beverly Hills, California.

Beverly Hills, California

Be.
Iconic.

But always
be LOVE.

Beverly Hills, California.

Beverly Hills, California.

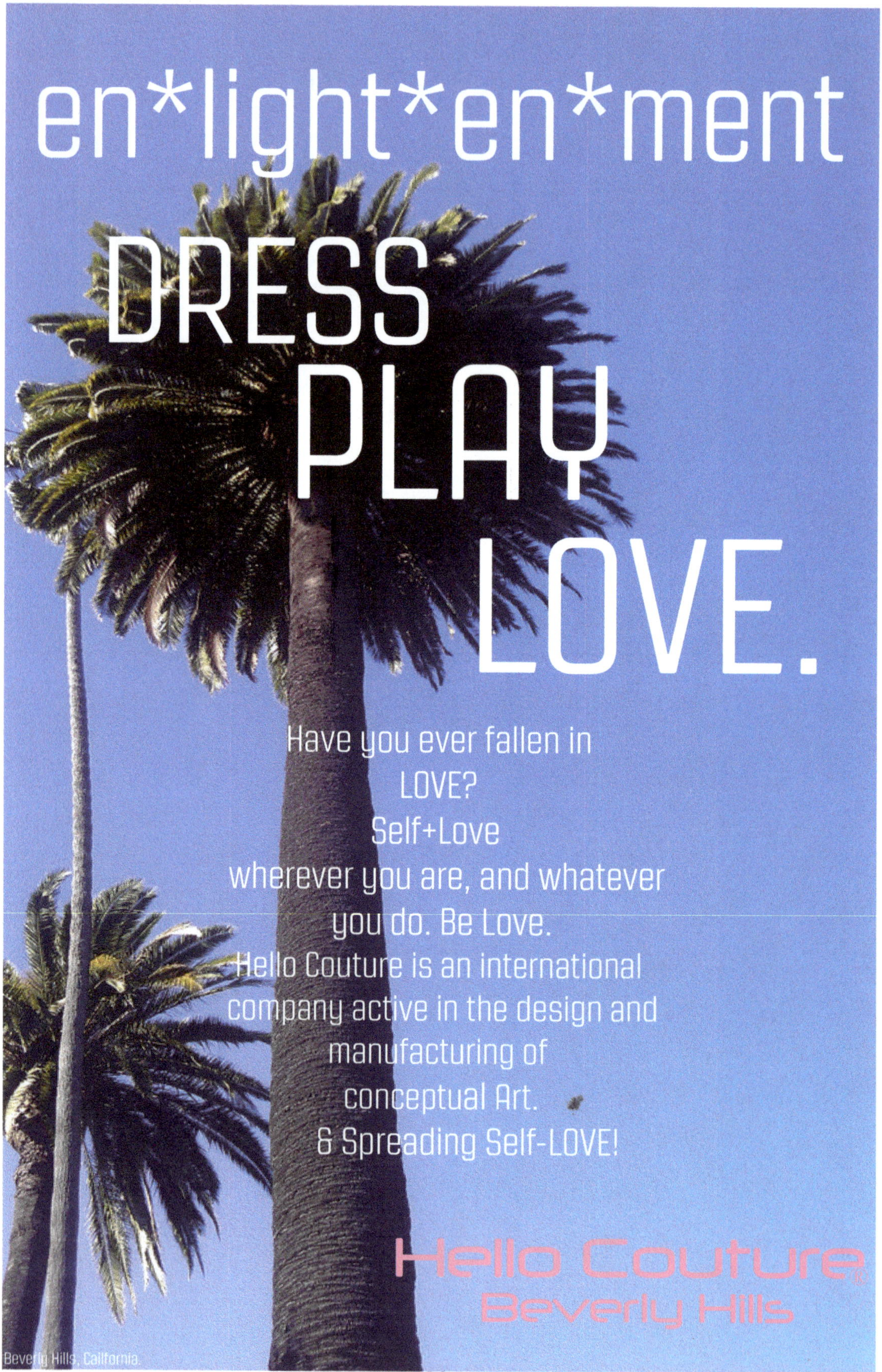

en*light*en*ment

DRESS
PLAY
LOVE.

Have you ever fallen in
LOVE?
Self+Love
wherever you are, and whatever
you do. Be Love.
Hello Couture is an international
company active in the design and
manufacturing of
conceptual Art.
& Spreading Self-LOVE!

Hello Couture
Beverly Hills

Beverly Hills, California.

South Beach Miami, Florida .

Beverly Hills, California.

MINDFULNESS
ARE YOU
PRESENT?

2ND TIME

Beverly Hills, California.

Beverly Hills, California.

Beverly Hills, California.

Beverly Hills, California.

Beverly Hills, California

Beverly Hills, California

Beverly Hills, California.

41

123

Beverly Hills, California.

Beverly Hills, California.

44

Beverly Hills, California.

Beverly Hills, California

Beverly Hills, California.

Chapter 2

HELLO

COUTURE

BOUQUET

#69

..AGE OF AQUARIUS, Love is the Lesson. Love & Light.

SPREAD UNcONDITIONAL LOVE.

Self+Love Unapologetically, don't care what people say or think, Fuck it! -Not everyone is open to unconditional love. Practice goodwill, and remember not to engage in negativity as it opens the door to and feeds/fuels chaos. Don't be petty, if you are unhappy with something or someone move on... Self-help is about being successful in the life you create for yourself and understanding who you are and also its understanding people, one of the simplest lessons is being nice and considerate of others. Do not let people control your emotions. Do not take actions in your own hands if you think you have been wronged by someone, even if you think your justified, the Universe and karma is aware, and has everyone's name. My Grandmother and Mother use to tell me "those that do negative actions all have karma coming there way, what people do not understand is it can be a small circle and other times it can be a large circle meaning years later" peace be upon you as karma is a bitch that never forgets to give harsh lessons. When you feel as if negativity outweighs the good or you have been wronged by someone never fret, dust yourself off and smile keep Good Vibes as the universe, yin and yang, the negative and positive, understand life is balance. We all have free will so when someone gives no fucks to this spiritual universal law the universe settles the score, payback hence karma. It's a powerful energy that is best avoided that is why it is best to just always be love, even if someone else doesn't dig it and is negative, ignore difuse do not react and have understanding that their is a reason for their negativity, donot let them drag you into feeding it. The universe is always watching. Be Love & Light. moveon... I proactively, and claim to self-love, make time for gratitude sessions, show gratitude, selfless service (an act of helping others without any thought of repayment in return) love everyone.

"LOVE THYSELF AND BE FORGIVING.
DON'T POINT FINGERS, AS YOU ARE THE
ARCHITECT OF YOUR LIFE
..AGE OF AQUARIUS, FEEL divine LOVE."

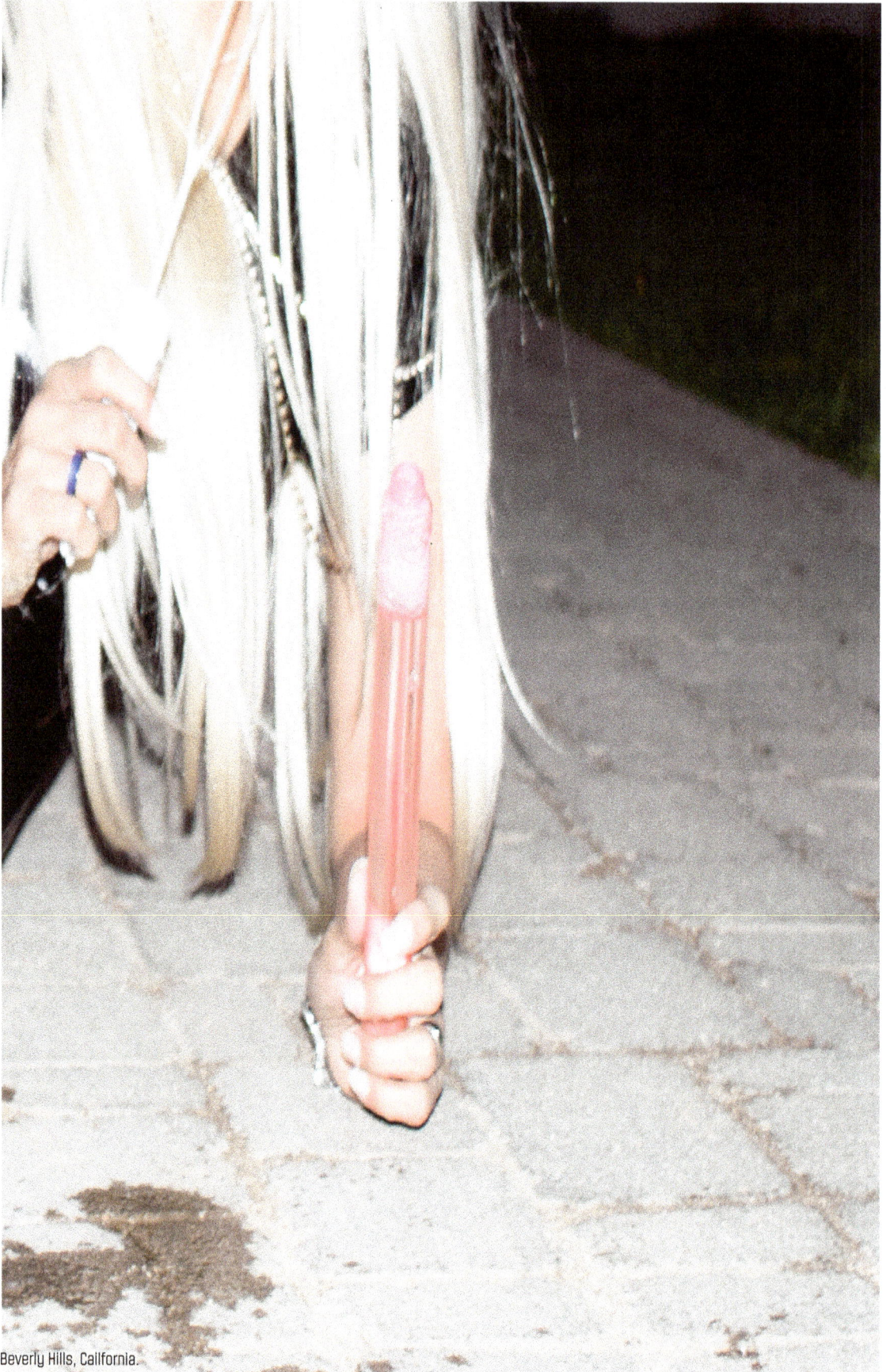

Beverly Hills, California.

Beverly Hills, California.

Beverly Hills, California.

Beverly Hills, California.

Tarzana, California.

Brentwood, Bel Air

Los Angeles, Cailfornia.

Los Angeles, California.

Beverly Hills, California

61

Lubov. Discover the first makeup made from sacred adornment & Fusing Rose Quartz Crystal powder.

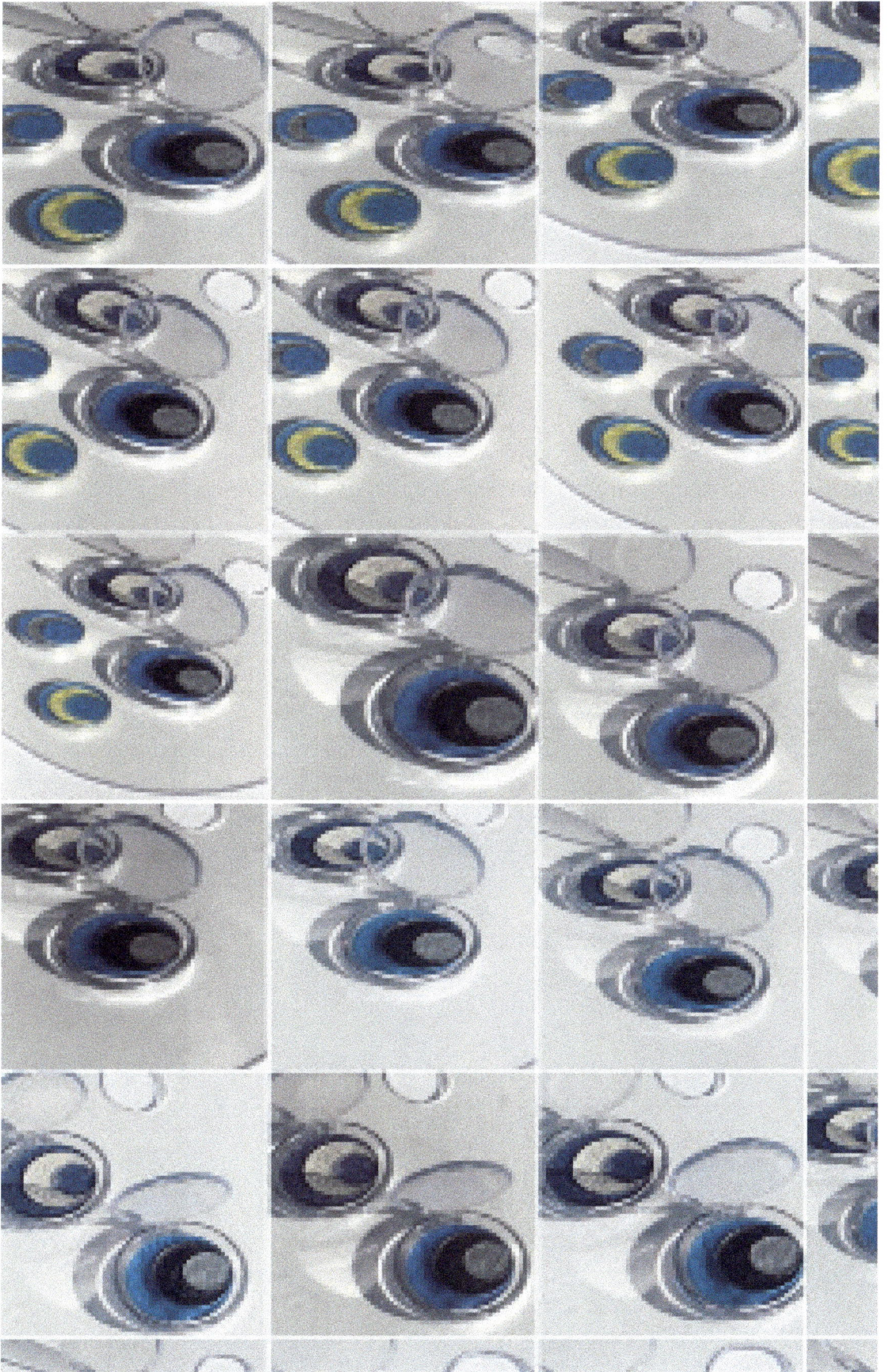

South Beach Miami, Florida.

South Beach Miami, Florida.

San Francisco, California.

South Beach Miami #405, Florida.

South Beach Miami #405, Florida.

South Beach iam #405, Florida.

TAKE WHAT YOU NEED.

Love.
Well-Being.
Integrity.
Dignity.
I.F.O.T.C.
Get Fucked.
Fidelity.
Cherry Cola.
Clarity.
Peace.

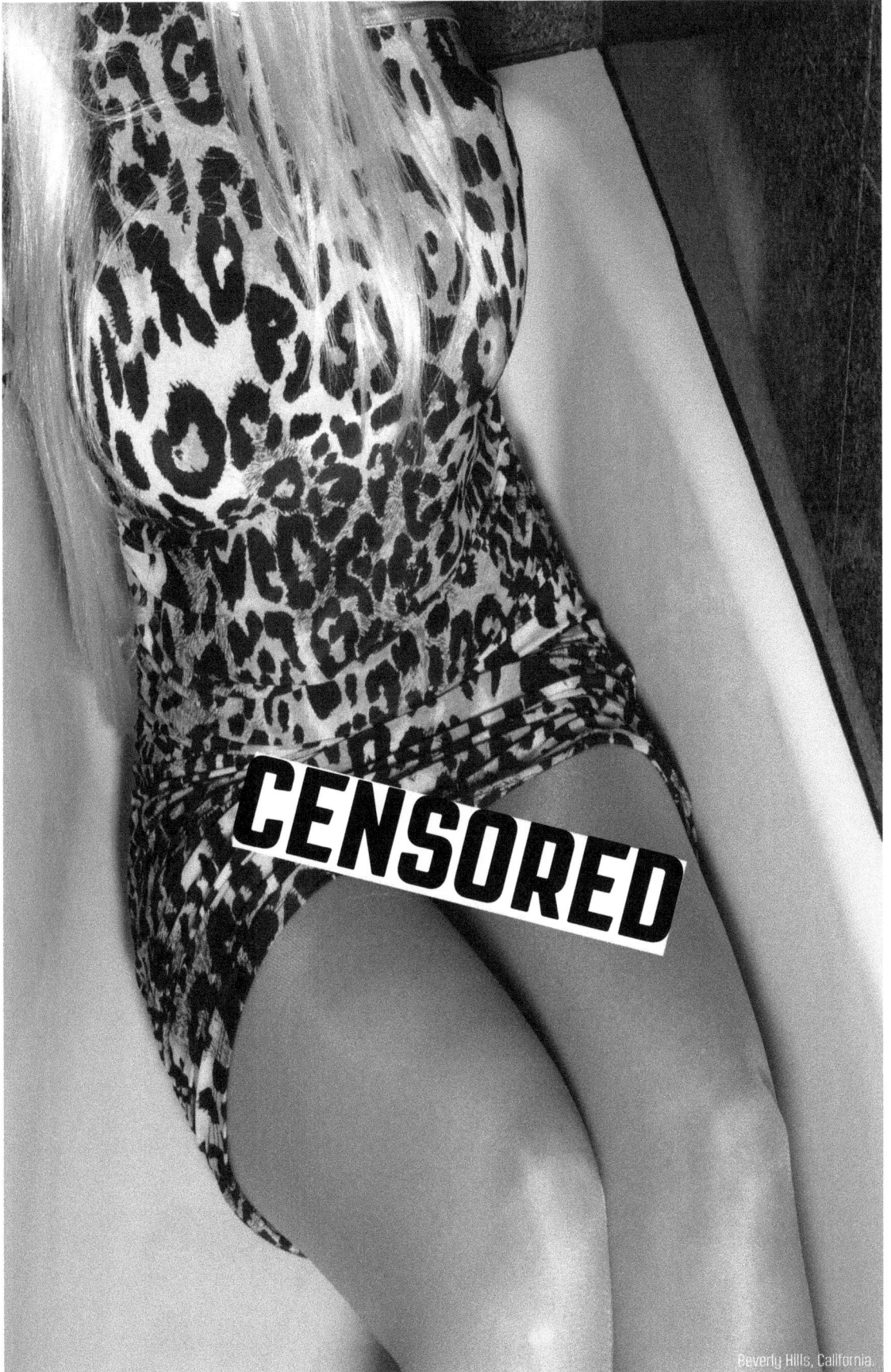

CENSORED

Beverly Hills, California.

Chapter 3

MINDFUL NESS

STRONG LOVE FORMULA
PLAY. GROW.
PLANT THE SEED, FERTILIZE, FEED,
NOURISH, CARE, WATER, PLAY
MUSIC, AND LOVE. THIS IS HOW YOU
GROW A PLANT.
THIS IS HOW YOU GROW SELF+LOVE
AND RELATIONSHIPS.
FIRST IT'S A SEED. (don't fight, to
young to Survive) THEN A PLANT. (Still
not Strong enough) THEN A BEAUTIFUL
STRONG TREE, YOU
NURTURE THE GROWTH.
we Are juSt like A plAnt

"WHEN YOU CULTIVATE YOUR SURROUNDINGS IN LOVE, LIFE IS A DETAILED KALEIDOSCOPE FILLED IN BLISSFUL BRILLIANT COLOURS AND TEXTURES."

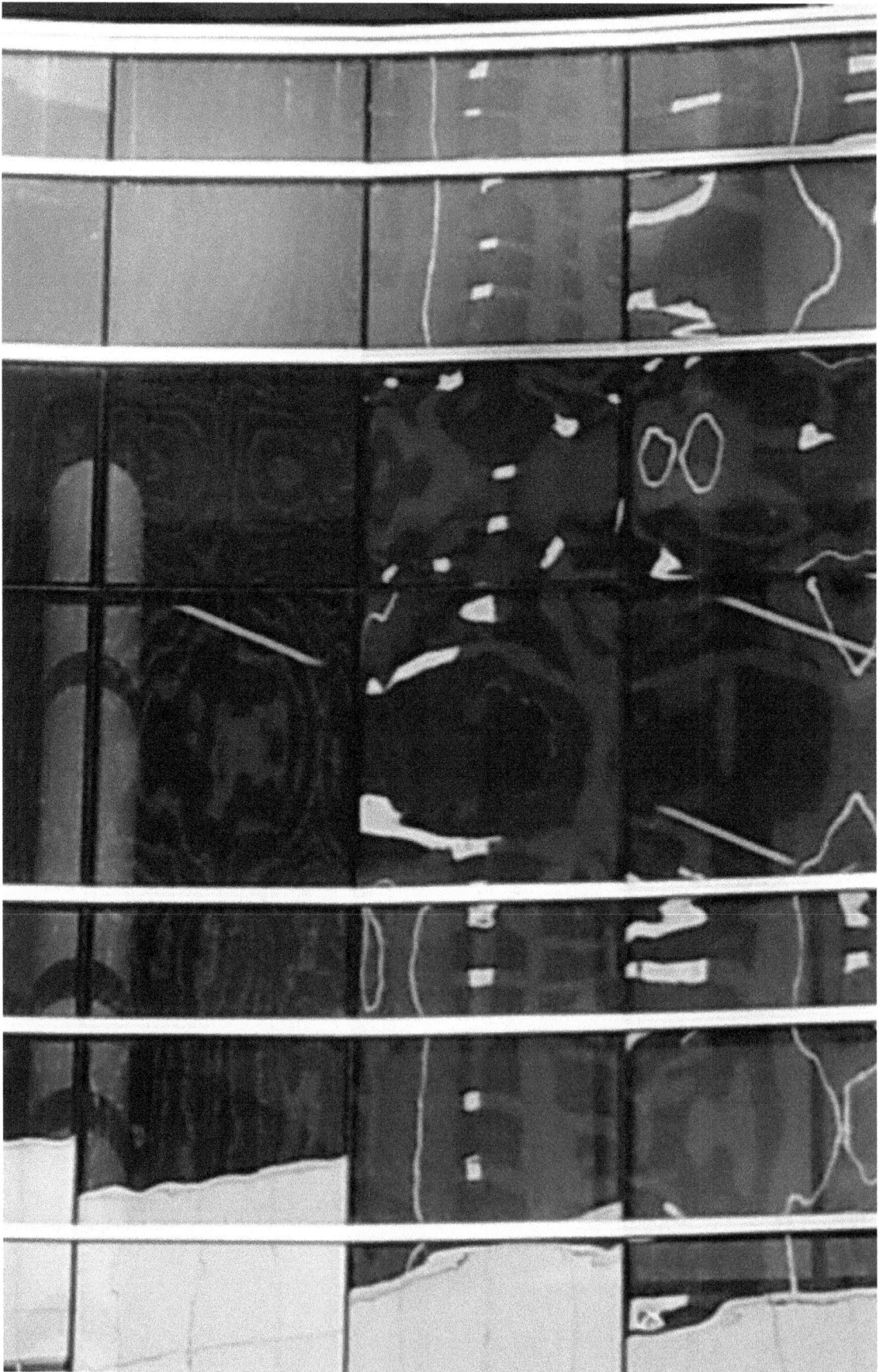

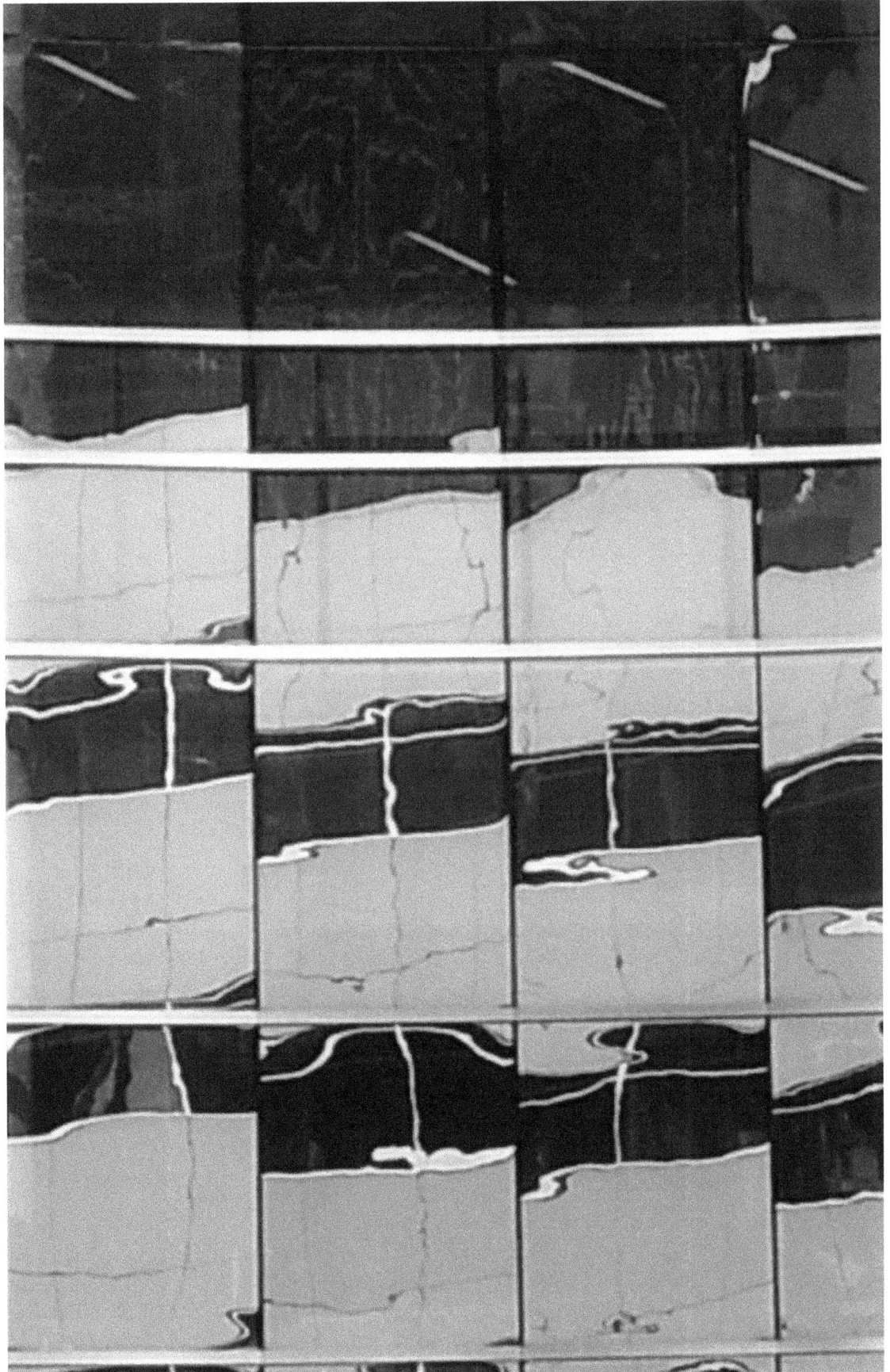

Catskill Mountains, New York.

Effingham, Illinois.

Palm Beach, Flordia.

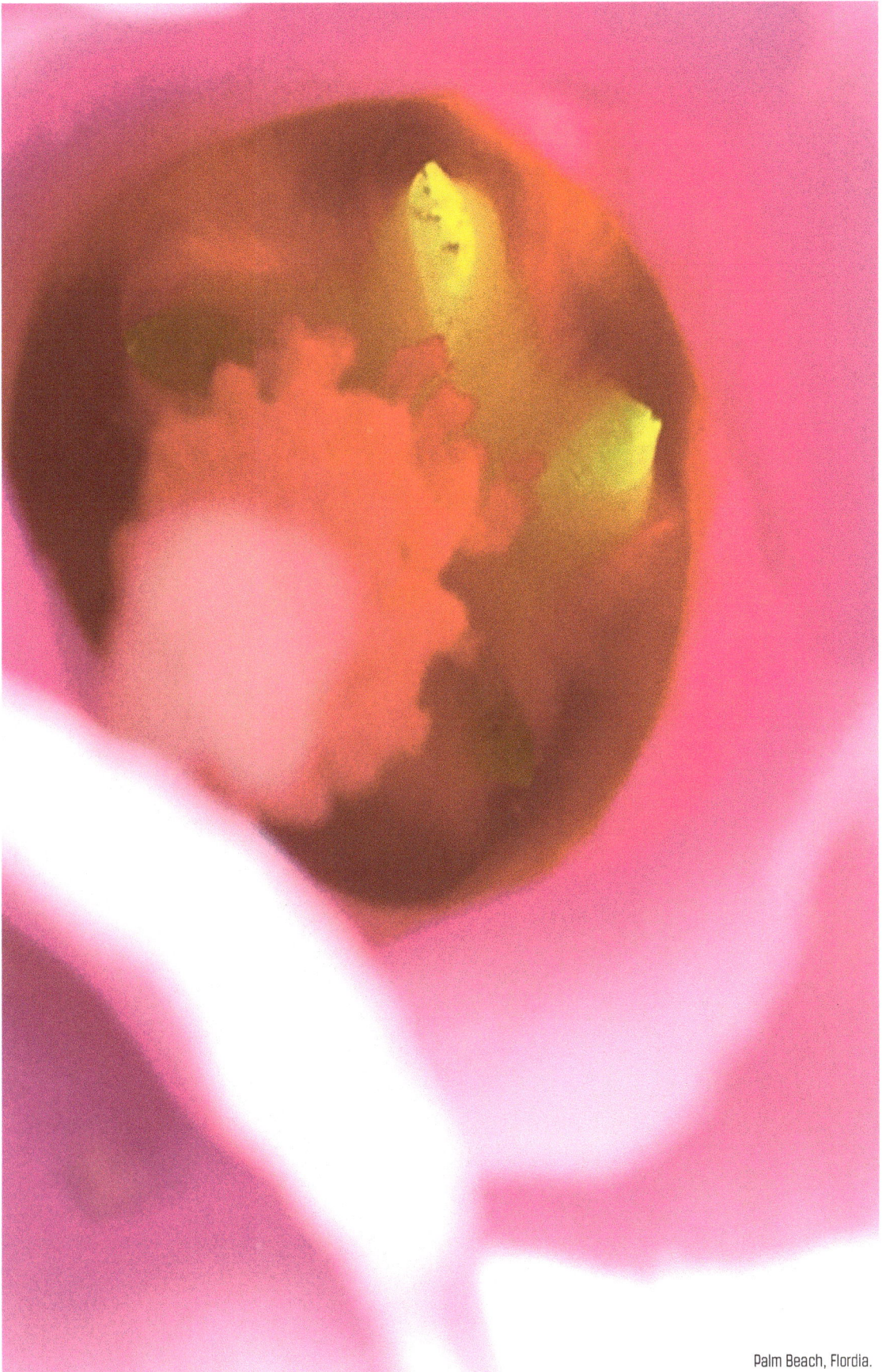

Palm Beach, Flordia.

Palm Beach, Flordia.

Orange Beach, Alabama.

Orange Beach, Alabama

Park City, Utah.

Park City, Utah.

Bethlem, Connecticut

Chapter 4

Fuck It..

I'm Just Going To
Wear
Red Lipstick

APRIL

I LOVE YOU TODAY, AND EVERYDAY.
I LOVE YOU TODAY, AND EVERYDAY.
I LOVE YOU TODAY, AND EVERYDAY.
I LOVE YOU TODAY, AND EVERYDAY.
I LOVE YOU TODAY, AND EVERYDAY.
I LOVE YOU TODAY, AND EVERYDAY.
I LOVE YOU TODAY, AND EVERYDAY.
I LOVE YOU TODAY, AND EVERYDAY.
I LOVE YOU TODAY, AND EVERYDAY.
I LOVE YOU TODAY, AND EVERYDAY.
I LOVE YOU TODAY, AND EVERYDAY.
I LOVE YOU TODAY, AND EVERYDAY.
I LOVE YOU TODAY, AND EVERYDAY.
I LOVE YOU TODAY, AND EVERYDAY.

SELF-LOVE

NOTE BOOK
mindfulness
JOURNAL

Write on me!

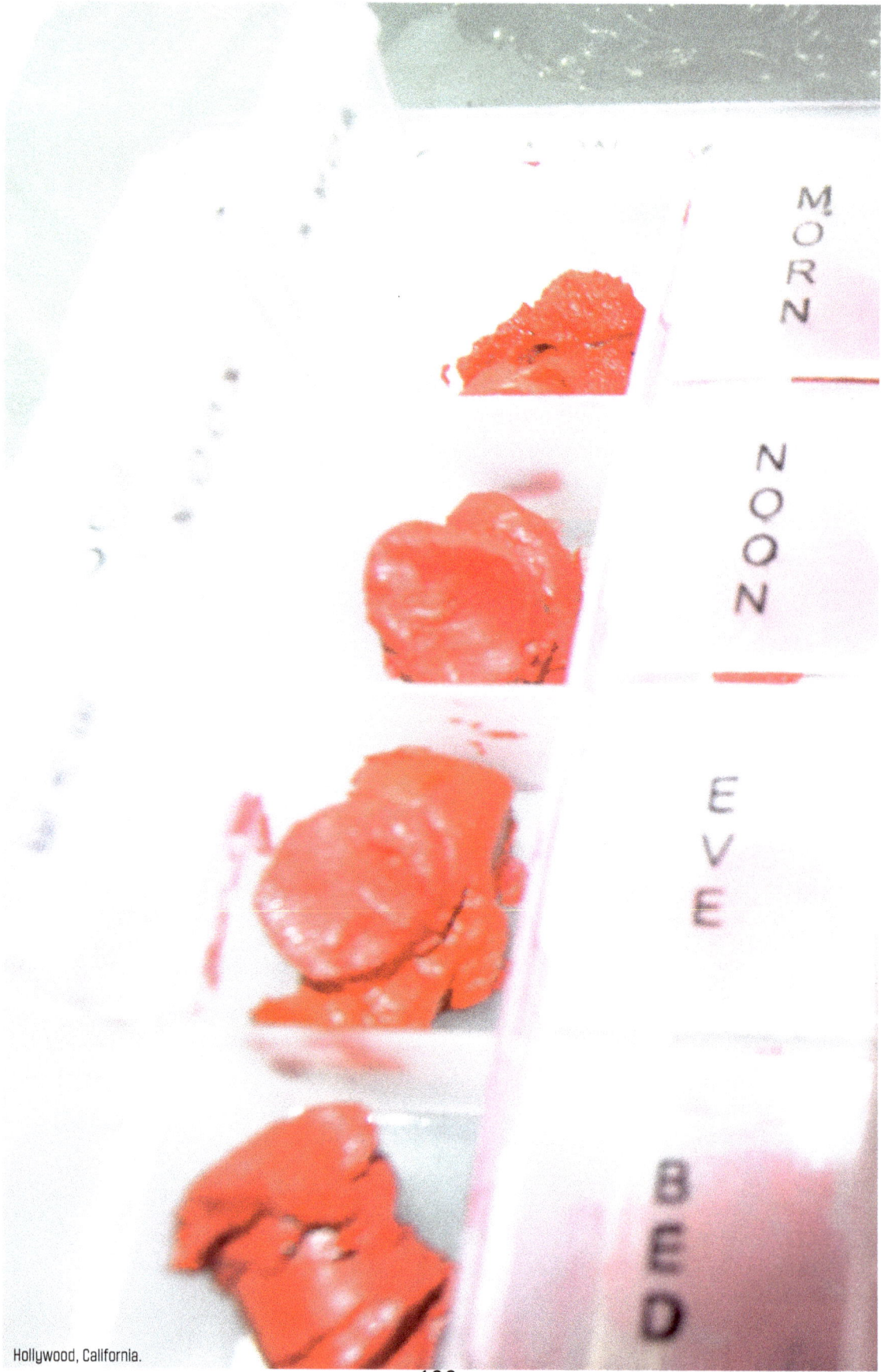

MORN

NOON

EVE

BED

Hollywood, California.

Hollywood, California.

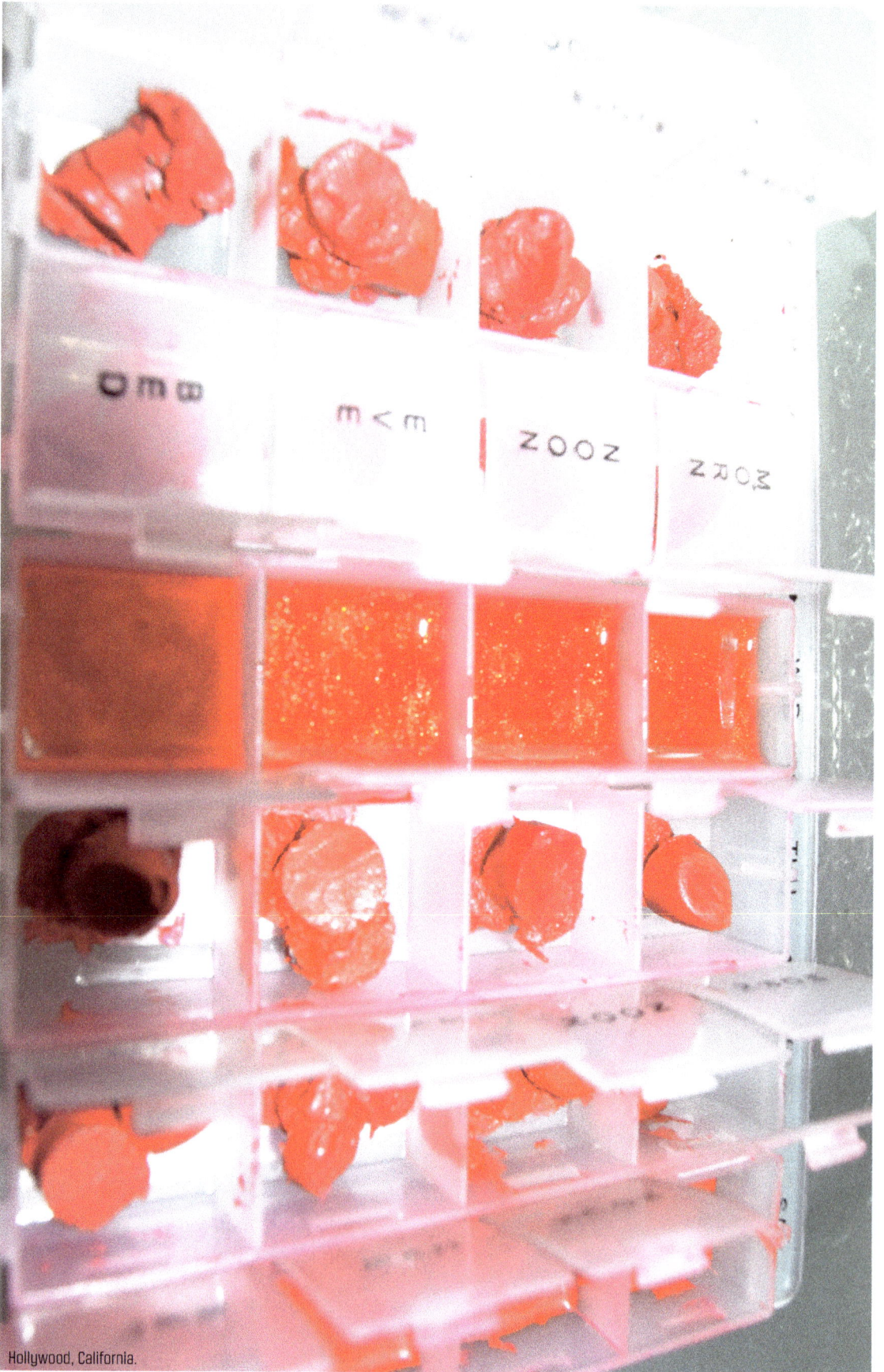

Hollywood, California.

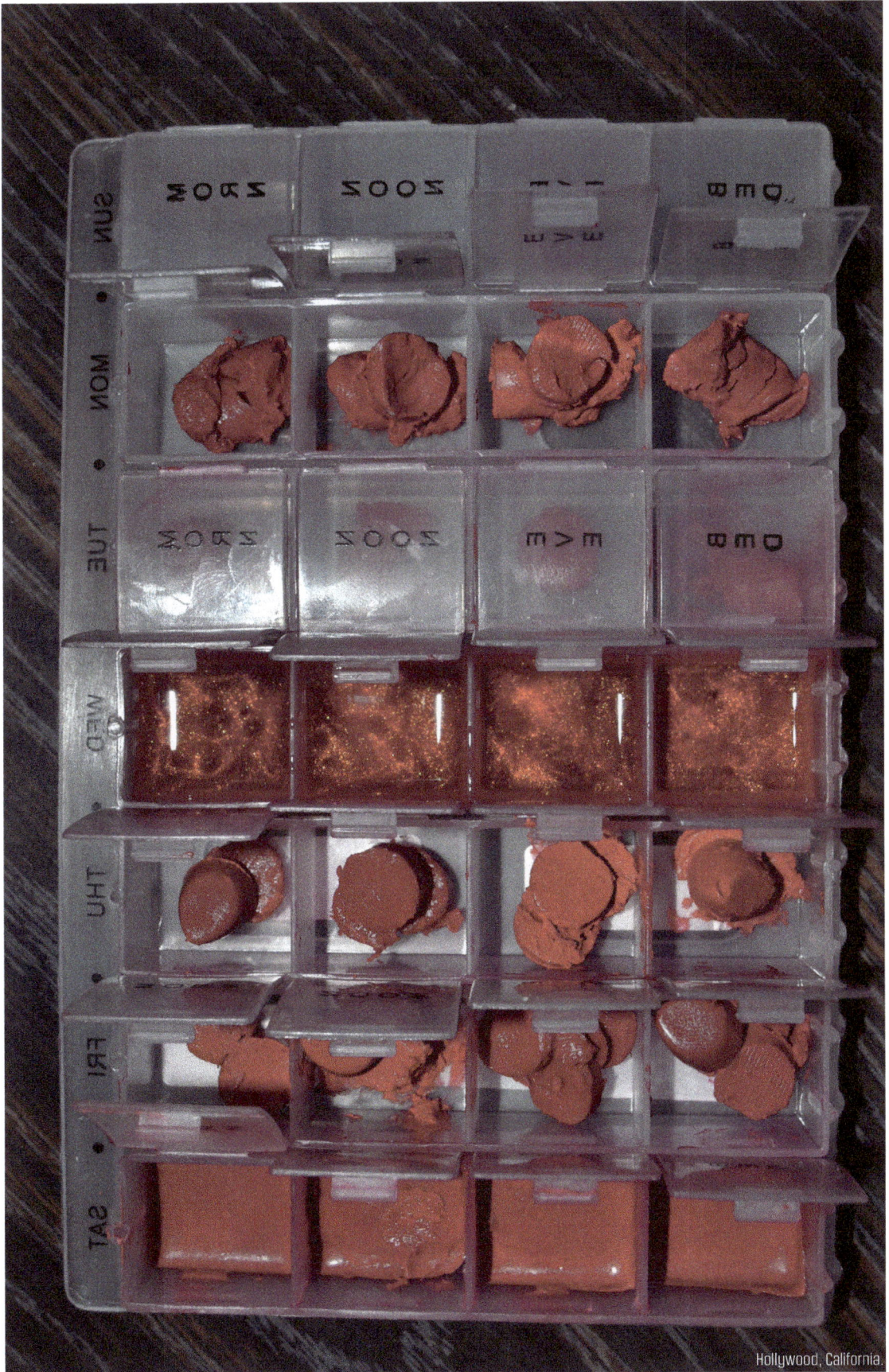

Hollywood, California.

STALKING IS SUCH A HARSH INTENSE RESEARCH OF A

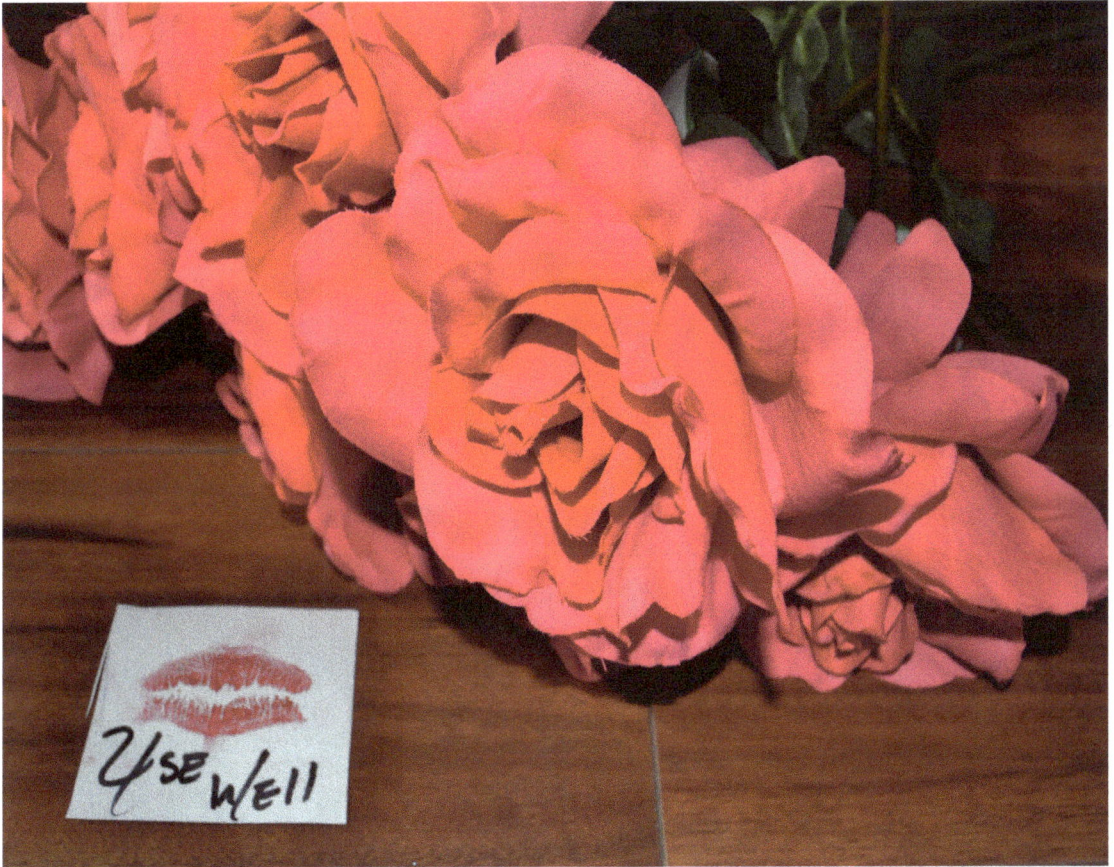

Use well

WORD. I LIKE TO VIEW IT AS INDIVIDUAL. STALK yourSELF

Los Angeles, California.

"NO MATTER HOW NICE YOU ARE, OR HOW HATEFUL YOU ARE, PEOPLE ARE GOING TO TRIP REGARDLESS. BE LOVE, BE YOURSELF, & SELF + LOVE."

"FUCK'EM JUST BE!"

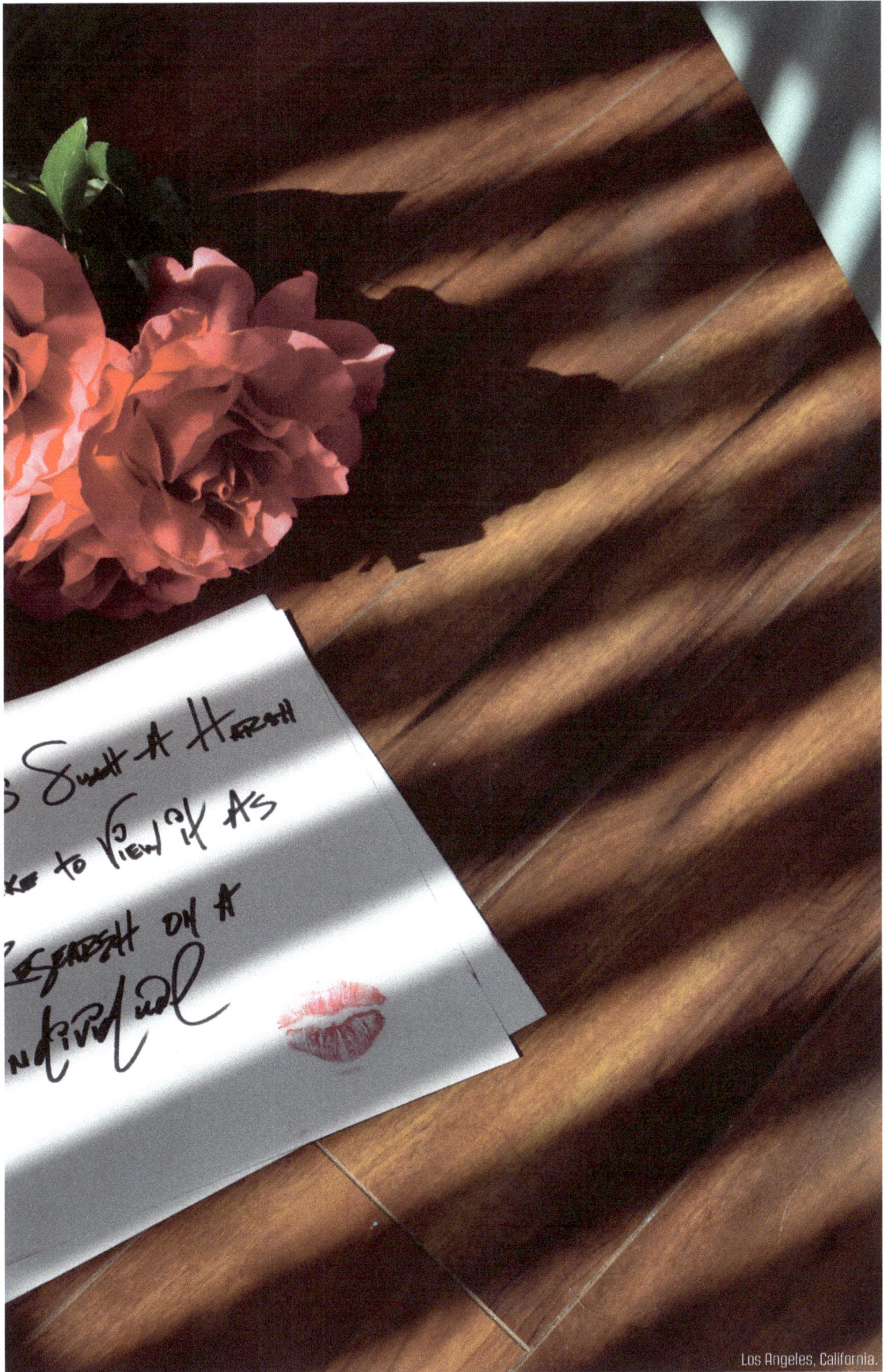

BE non-judgemental.

Be unapologetically yourself.

We live in a Culture that defines what beauty is
suppose to look like, the good news is... humanity is making
a positive radiCal Change by evolving. Have you looked at
soCial media and publiCation's? we are evolving but we
still have a long way to go. Thanks to the millennials
with their moXie and forward thinking. What use to be
Considered different and unorthodoX
beauty is now the manifestation birth of the IConiC.
Beautiful, and epiC beauty! We are all beautiful.
SoCiety's progressive movement deserves more ConsCious
awareness to let us all Be authentiC and to grow this message universally.
We truly are all unique and beautiful.
Be unapologetiCally yourself. Be non-judgemental.
Have understanding of someone's aesthetiC. Be supportive.
RespeCt everyone's truth as everyone of us has our own
freewill we all deserve to take our own unique and beautiful
path/journey to be. be-nonjudgemental of

someone's journey, and love all.

How to be a good friend to yourself.

working with our inner+self/CritiC.
Be loving. Tell yourself, daily I Love you! FoCus
only on the positive. Live in the present let go
of the past. You deserve to LOVE yourself.
YOU deserve LOVE.

Brentwood, California. Flower Outside Marilyn Monroe's last home.

Brentwood, California. Flower Outside Marilyn Monroe's last home.

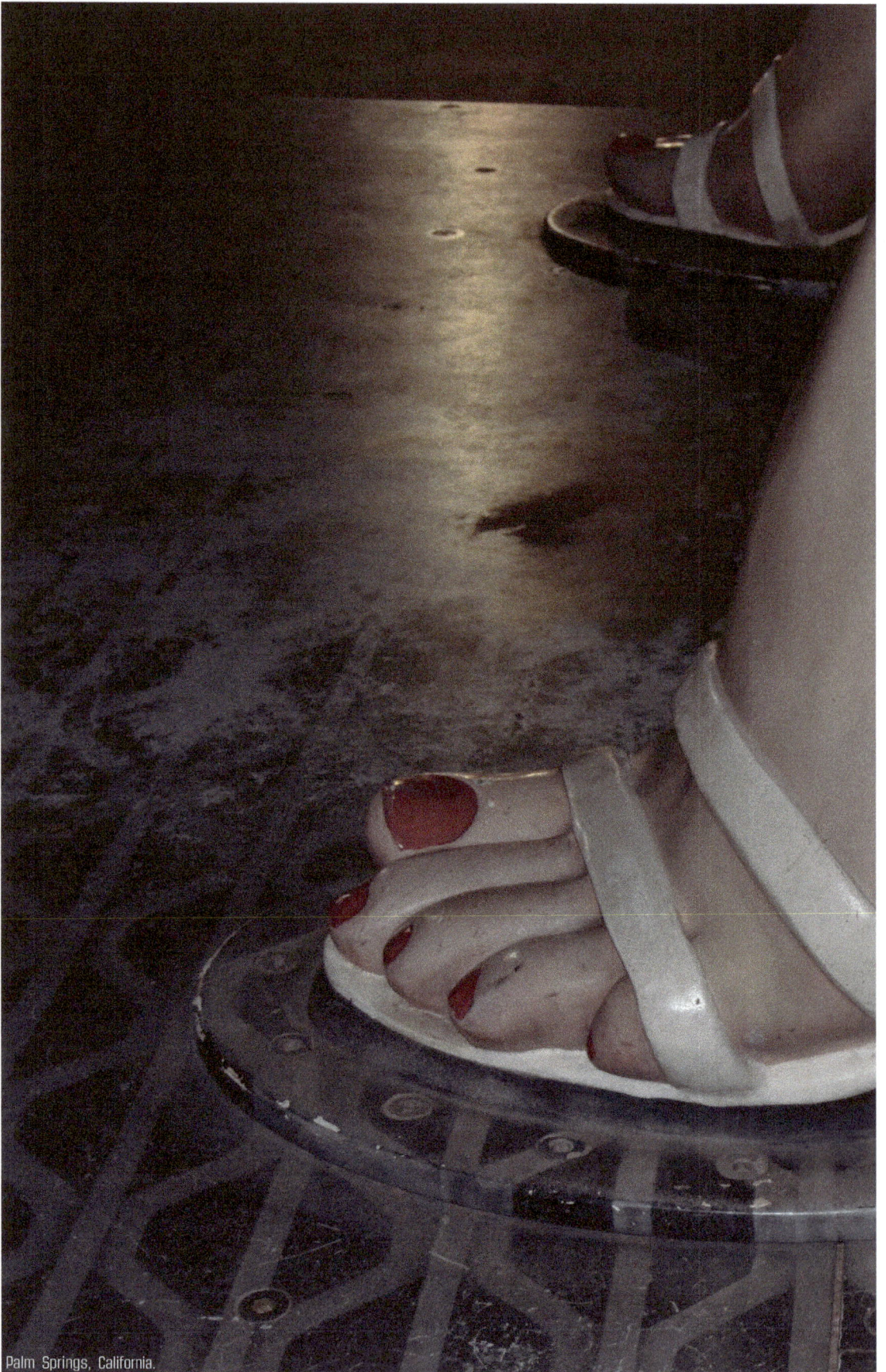

Palm Springs, California.

Palm Springs, California.

116

Palm Springs, California.

UNFUCK YOURSELF

In order to reCeive we must open our auriC field/astral light and
must be Cleansed and empowered and the soul fed.
Cleaning our energy, washing away negativity, and enhanCing
our psyChiC gifts.

Grocery List
16 ounCes eaCh of CoConut water, and milk.
8 ounCes CoConut sugar.
1 ounCe florida water or any natural perfume.
1 bottle of Holy water (has powerful intention
energy/vibrations of blessings, proteCtion)
1 natural CoConut soap
2 selenite stone rounded shape flat shape about
   5 inChes in length. (selenite Crystals are soluble in
   water, do not be alarmed if it dissolves in water)
1 seven day Candle.
8 drops of Cold Compressed Olive Oil.

THE BATH
always take a shower first to rid yourself of impurities before a
ritual bath.
Cleansing. Purify your aura. ProteCt your auriC fields.
This bath also rids yourself of other peoples negative vibrations
that you have been in CONTACt with or and anyone sending
not good vibes.

For best results take this Cleanse at night.

ote: no salt for this bath as this deity that gave this
ath dislikes salt. This is a sweet bath. and Calm's the mind.

tent. Cleansing the mind, body and Cleansing the spirit.

ake this bath at night before bed.
 draw bath luke warm not hot on the Cooler side.
 tub half way.
 light Candle add three drops of olive oil inside.
 add 8 drops of olive oil, all of the perfume. pour half the
 gredients into the bath water.
 immerse yourself in water. Chill for 8 minutes while
olding your selenite in each hand. don't worry if it gets wet as it is
placeable and wants to do its job of dispelling negativity, i want
ou to think of nothing and be Calm as spirit is aware what your
tent is and wants you to destress.
 slowly pour the rest of the Contents unto your Crown Chakra.
 let your body air dry.
 dress white in a Clean white t-shirt and Cover your Crown Chakra
ith a Cotton sCarf. all white for purity.
 sleep with Clean white sheets. shower in the morning.
 plaCe Candle some where that is higher than your head.
t it burn until it is done.

Never leave a burning Candle unattended.

Chapter 5

i Want 2 Marry You

MAY

Meditation on Gratitude

write what you are grateful for... turn negativity into positive.
See the beauty in everything even thorns in roses...

Write on me!

"GRATITUDE JOURNAL."

Danberry Fair mall Carnival, Connecticut.

Danberry Fair mall Carnival, Connecticut.

Route 66 Arcadia, Oklahoma.

Route 66 Arcadia, Oklahoma.

Cleanse your aura with flowers.... put them in your bath.

Las Vegas, Nevada.

Las Vegas, Nevada.

Mandeville, Louisiana.

Las Vegas, Nevada.

Chicago, Illinois.

Beverly Hill's Grass
infused with CBD Oil.

raise your vibration.

Fontana, California.

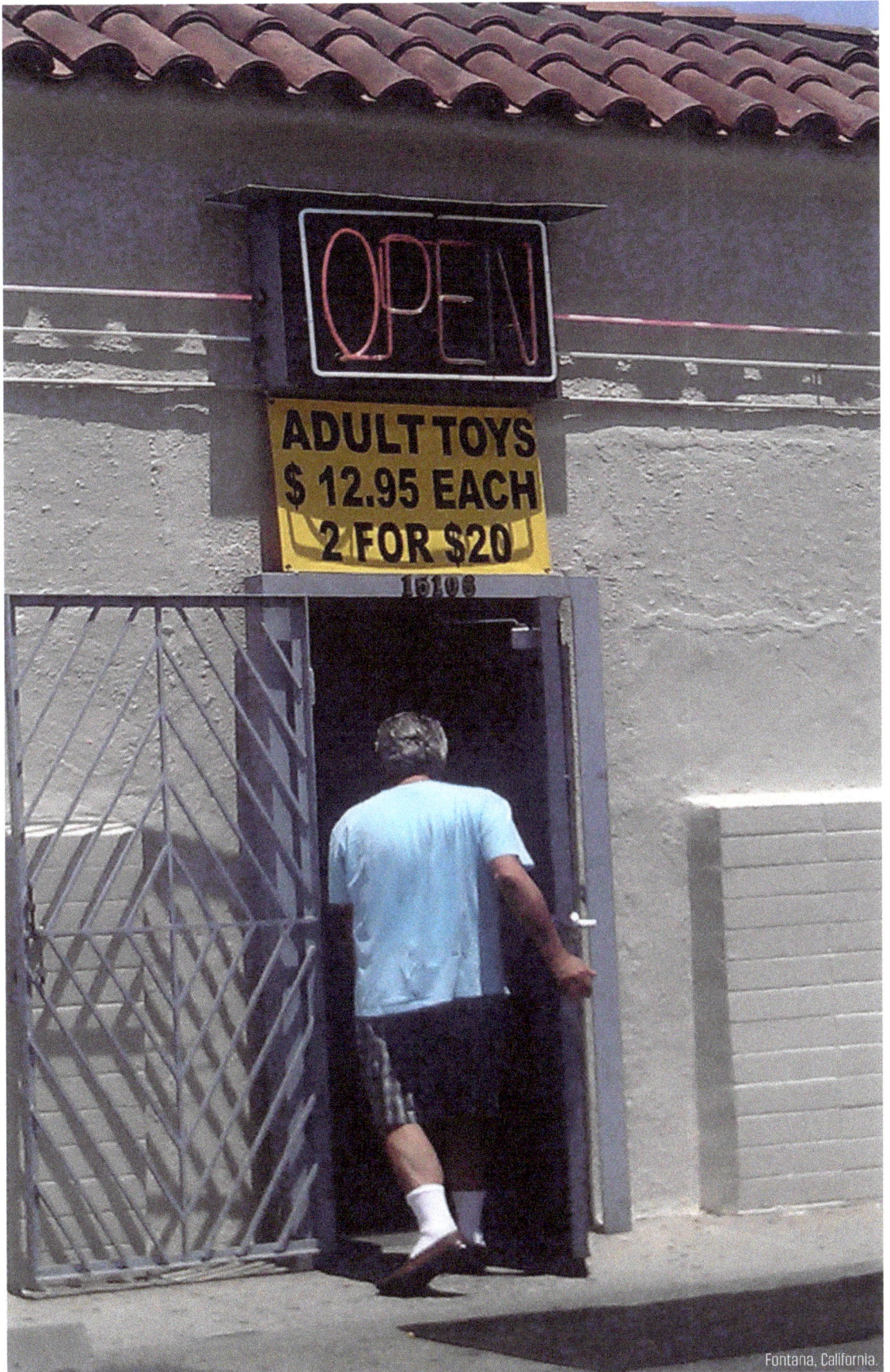

OPEN

ADULT TOYS
$ 12.95 EACH
2 FOR $20

Fontana, California.

Widener, Arkansas.

136

Widener, Arkansas.

Be Present. Live. <small>stay there.</small>

Whilst wearing Glitter at a Music Festival and allowing yourself to play. <small>take a deep breath/inhale. breathe out.</small>

SELF-Love is feeding our body, mind, and spirit. <small>tune into your bodies sensations.</small>

Love is an energy, tap into pure energy flow at a musiC festival. Sometimes it is enlightening to pla Splash your body in glitter.

they say going to live music shows lengthens your life, rises feelings of wellbeing.

Glitter Los Angeles, California..

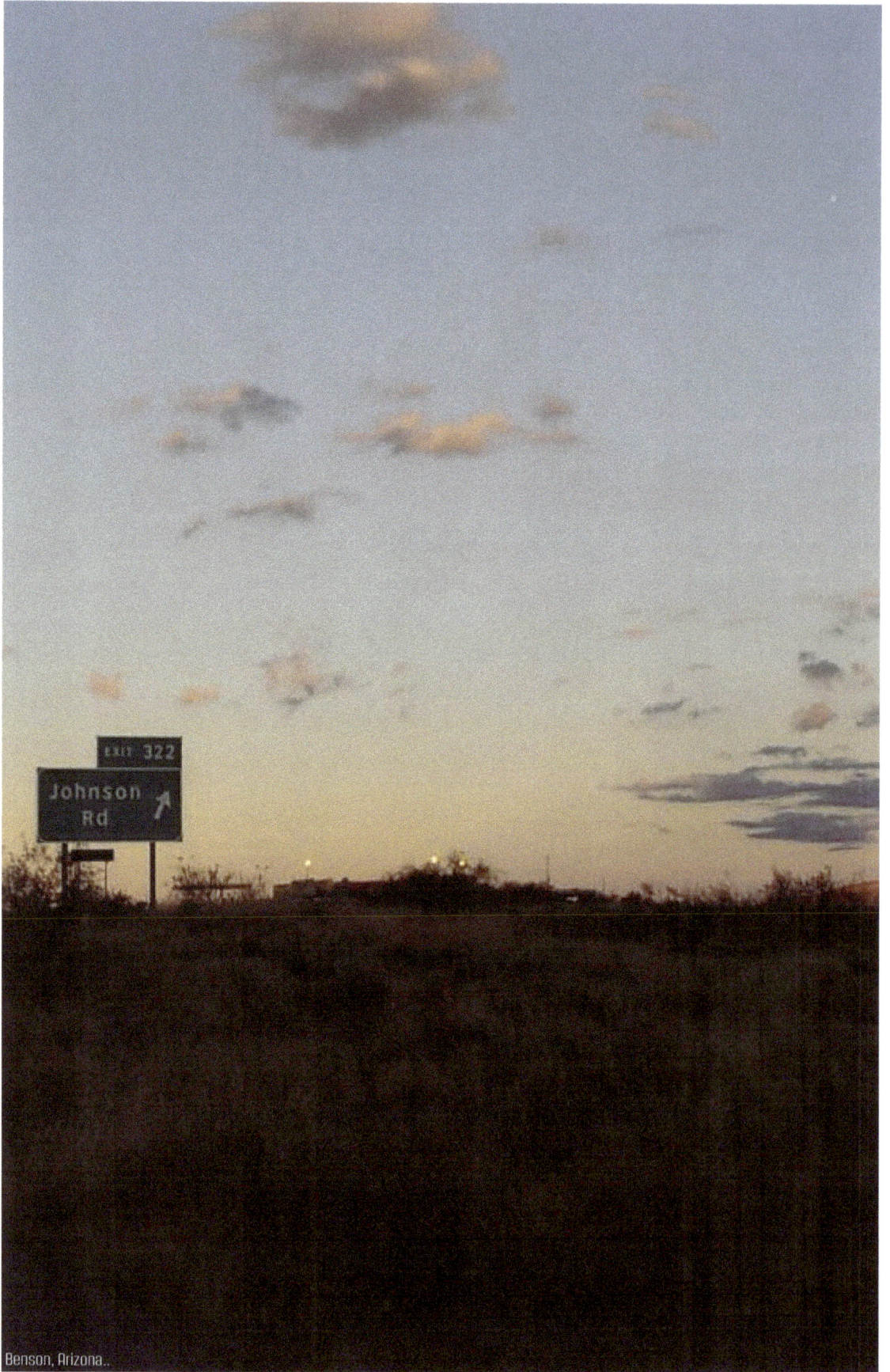

EXIT 322

Johnson
Rd

Benson, Arizona..

Chapter 6

WET

JUNE

BE PEACEFUL, ALWAYS LOVE AND SHOW LOVE. TEST YOURSELF BY FORGIVING SOMEONE THAT YOU THINK HAS WRONGED YOU AND MOVE ON AND LET IT GO.

be the Change. unConditional love.

AuthentiC spirituality is always forgiving, being spiritual is having an understanding of human behavior that no one is perfeCt. Life is a journey of getting to know ourselves and tapping into the Divine. Have Compassion for those that haven't reaChed the higher state of being by not engaging in petty and judgemental behavior, no one is jusitified in engaging in tit -or -tat behavior as we are not...

G_d / SourCe / Creator

beautiful.

you Cannot argue about taste or beauty... Regardeless of how muCh or little makeup you wear means nothing if you don't feel beautiful within and feel Confident about yourself. We all have our own beauty, find yours. mirror meditation.....spend time in the mirror looking at yourself finding who you are...we are all beautiful in our own way no one is unattraCtive it's someone's negative

behavior that makes them undesirable. Be Comfortable in your own skin, disCover the BEAUTIFUL YOU!

Just FOR FUN...remember to have fun, in life.

i want you to feel beautiful, feel seXy & find your mojo. Do things that are fun and uninhibited at your own Comfort level.
its the summer..FOR THE SUMMER

SHAKE YOUR HAIR OUT, TREAT YOURSELF TO AN OVER THE TOP LUXURIOUS FOUR-INCH fuCk ME HIGH HEELS. (make sure you treat yourself on a regular basis don't wait just for the summer to splurge) INDULGE.

Thi month, be as FINE CULTIVATED WINE GRAPES Ready to be organiCally RAVISHED. TASTE, DESIRE AND be PASSIONate about your life... as wine tastes better with age,

everyday Cultivate to learn and grow and beCome a better person. Taste it! Taste life, it's

deliCious.

LIVE. & LOVE.

when you live life in the realm of awakening. being present. mindfulness. gratitude. virtue. (self) Compassion. Love. Opening yourself to growth. the journey. the beauty of humanity, nature, tapping into the ConsCiousness of the divine "you" it is satisfying and fulfilling. You are never alone. you will find your authentic SOUL MATE within yourself, that you are enough. Life is a kaleidoscope of beauty. Life is beautiful when you are awake. Be present.

Santa Fe, New Mexico.

Santa Fe, New Mexico.

Santa Fe, New Mexico.

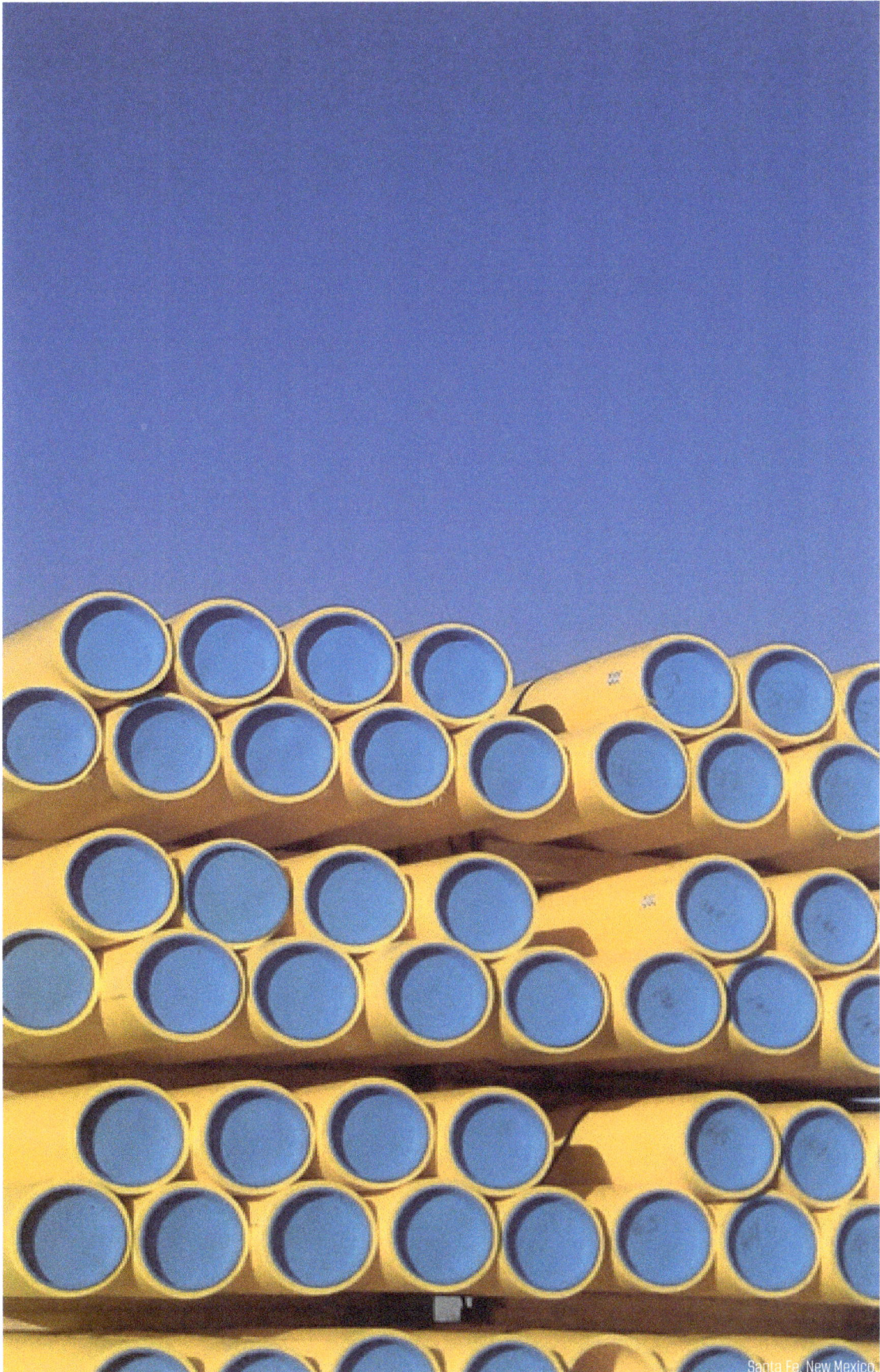

Santa Fe, New Mexico

New York City, New York.

Self-Care
CheCklist.
the answers are always within...

write your list on this page my Love's.

George Washington Bridge, New York.

George Washington Bridge, New York.

New York, New York

New York, New York.

East River, New York.

New York, New York.

Central Park South, New York.

Central Park South, New York.

Central Park South, New York.

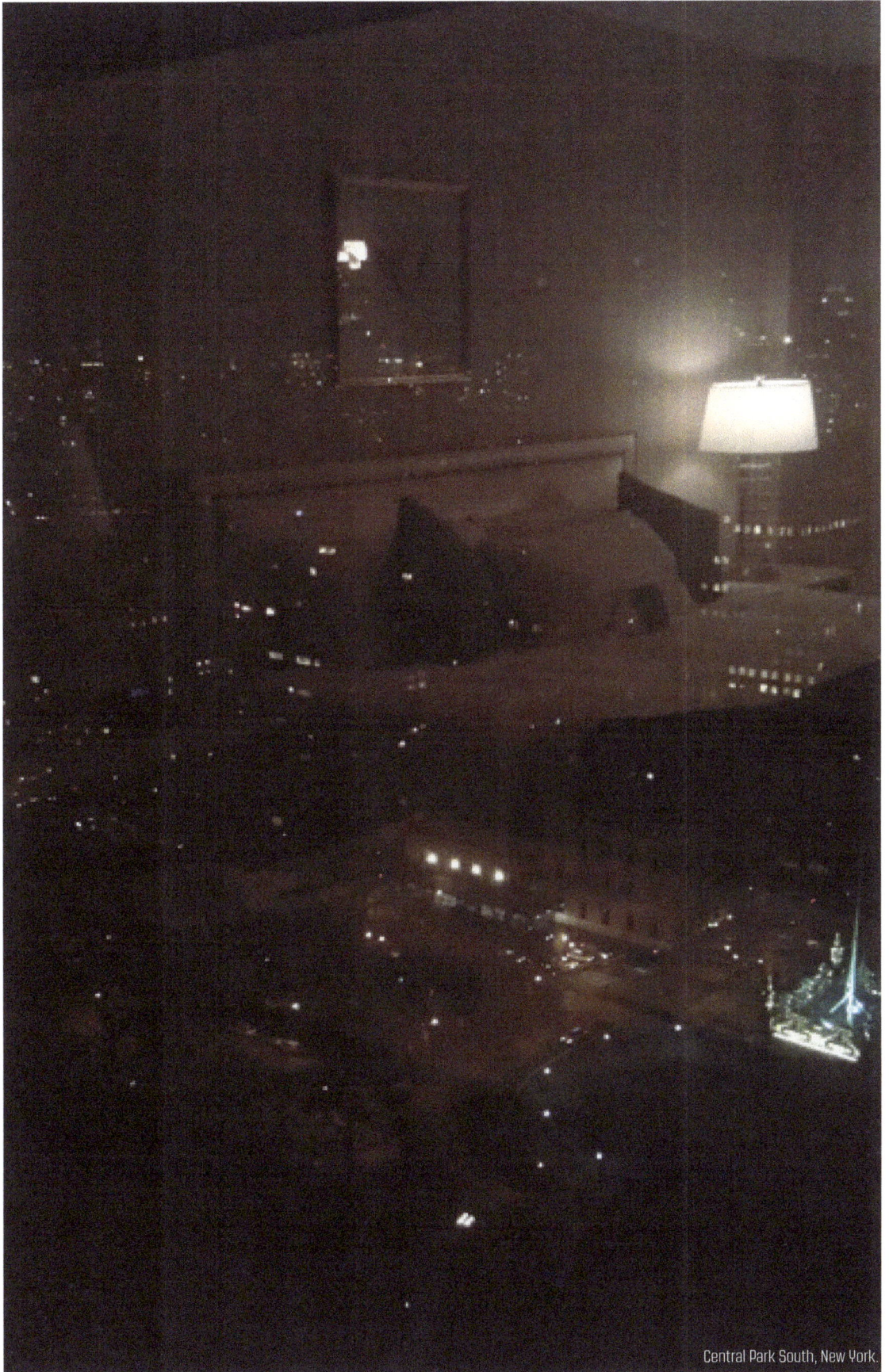
Central Park South, New York.

Chapter 7

Goddess Dust

& Wildflowers

JULY

INTENT. LOVE and NOURISHMENT. GO RAW. GUILT-FREE INDULGENCE..

WHY ARE YOU SO AFRAID OF NATURE AND GARDENS?
Nature and gardens remind us that we need to nourish and love ourselves, in order to grow and bloom.

EXPLORE. NATURE WALK...Forge mushrooms, pick WILD FLOWERS. VISIT YOUR LOCAL SUSTAINABLE ORGANIC FARMS.
indulge In... extraordinary FRESH VEGETABLES AND FRUIT.
FAST ON RAW FRUIT & VEGGIES FOR 48 HOURS. Drink RAW WATER.

saCred. you are saCred. treat yourself as the divine being that you are...
get in touCh with yourself.
give yourself permission to be open, relax, enjoy, play and

reCeive Love. date yourself. Listen to your favorite musiC.
meditate. wear something or nothing at all that makes you feel beautiful and sexy AF! DanCe naked.
Be Comfortable in your own skin.

Raw LOVE and NOURISHMENT

Catskill Mountains, New York.

Catskill Mountains, New York.

Catskill Mountains, New York.

Catskill Mountains, New York

171

Catskill Mountains, New York.

Catskill Mountains, New York.

Ventura County, California

Ventura County, California

Nashville, TN.

Nashville, TN.

Laramie, Wyoming.

Laramie, Wyoming.

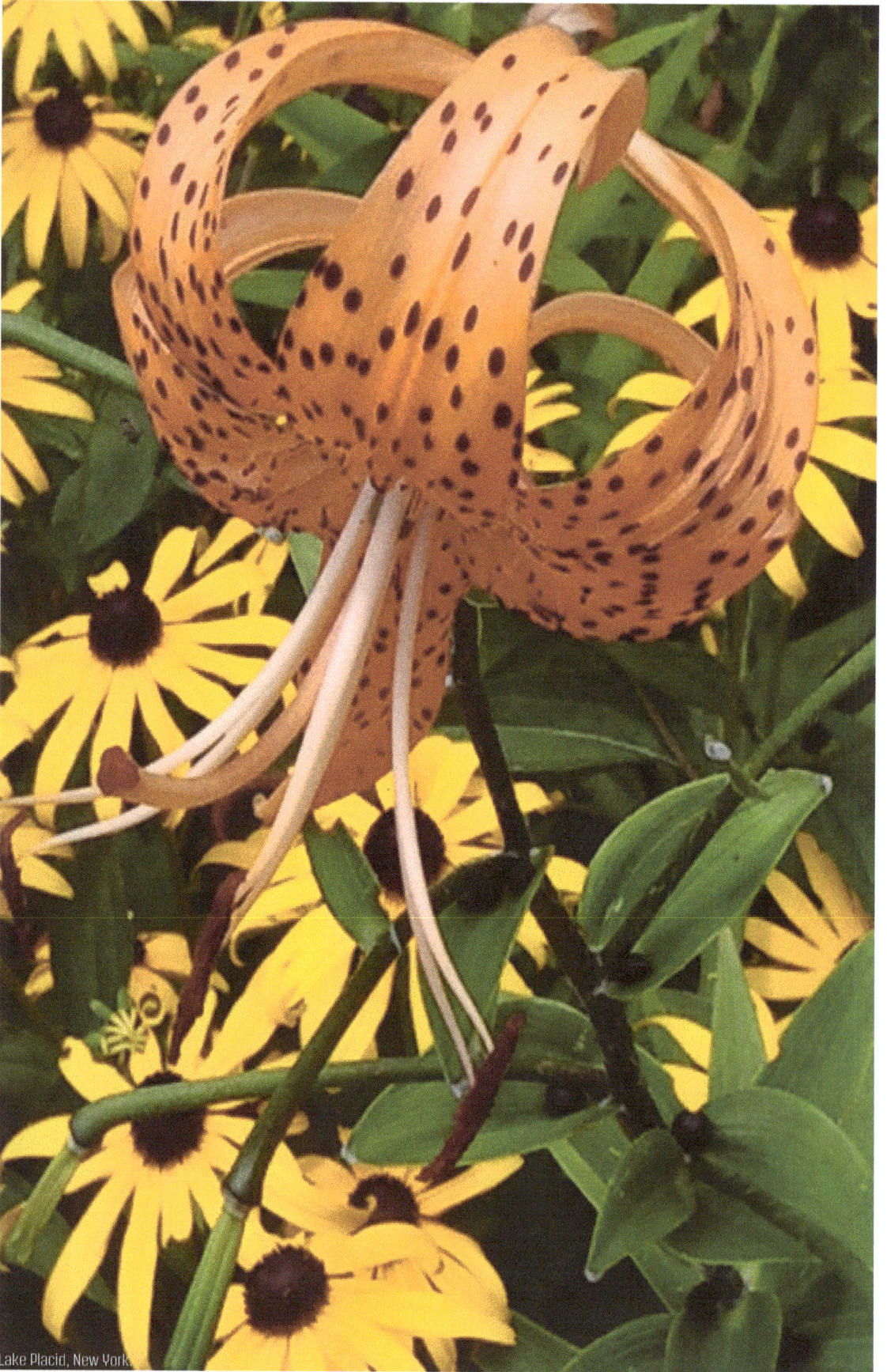

Lake Placid, New York.

180

Lake Placid, New York

Savannah, Georgia.

Savannah, Georgia.

Chapter 8

Fetish Garden

AUGUST

VIBRATE with SUN. LOVE. ENERGY . . . . . OSHUN. VENUS. APHRODITE.

It's the peek of the SUMMER... you deserve to get in touch with your body, get in touch with nature. Learn to unplug at times. Get an alarm Clock so the first thing you do in the morning, is not look at a your digital deviCEs. Everything has a vibration, everything has a energy. tap into the Clean energy of the sun and the love.

goddess . . . . . OSHUN

Take a trip to the river. the River is a hypnotiC plaCe.

1. Bring Clean white Clothing.

2. Lubov (love) Rose water: With intention of Cleansing and to reCeive blessings of beauty, love and manifesting positive vibrations. Choose five organiC roses put yellow rose petals in a glass bowl, 5 Cups of raw water, then gently muddle, transfer into a glass mason jar with lid. Do not boil as you want live raw energy/vibrations from the rose. Let it steep under the sun rays before moonlight bring indoors and let it steep over night by your Rose Quartz. do during when the night is going to be a new full moon or when the moon is in venus.

3. Go to the river meditate on your intentions.

4. Cleasing: after meditation give an offering to the deity of the river OSHUN, pour Pink or any fine Champagne into the water as she loves it! 5 tsp. powdered Cinnamon, always taste the honey as their

is a pakti that someone tried to poison her (for vegans use vegan honey) first give to her and then take

Care of your Yoni, rub onto your "MagiC Pussy" genitalia (power and love to everyone we all have "MagiC Genitalia" this is to awaken sensuality, align, and we need to keep this area unbloCked from negativity and Cleanse it with good vibrations) in a CirCular motion CloCkwise asking her to sweeten your life, and to Cleanse you, taking in the energy of Divine Feminine ArChetype OSHUN. Bathe naked in the river water, meditating on your intent. intentions.....

5. Dress in Clean white Clothes for the day also sleep in white. shower the following day. Offerings here are some ideas for offerings; Gold, Diamonds, Copper, honey, Cinnamon, Oranges, pumkins, yellow flowers, sunflowers. I also always give five pennies, these are a few things to give her as an offering from your heart out of love for her..... for blessings. Yet, my spirit guides are telling me for your first time bring five Sunflowers as OSHUN'S number is five and its multiples. Also if you Can plant yellow Daffodils by the river where it shall reCeive water, this symbol is for rebirth and new beginings, a gift for her and giving baCk to nature.....Make sure you don't disturb the balanCe of the loCal ECosystem area/Community that you are in....Please researCh before doing so.

Optional The Proper Option: Collect this raw water in a glass vessel. To drink. Use the raw water to bathe with at home. Cleanse Yoni; eggs, beads, stones, et Cetera set in your in your window or baCkyard under the sun, moon, and stars for 24 hours Yoni; eggs, beads, stones, eCetera as the results are FuCking Fabulous!

This OSHUN Cleansing: Blessings of self-love, love, attraCtion, beauty, money and wealth.

LOVE.
MaGIC

Be a vessel of Love..... Channel your Inner Love Goddess

New York, New York.

New York, New York.

Los Angeles,California.

Los Angeles, California.

BEST MEAL AFTER SEX.

90210

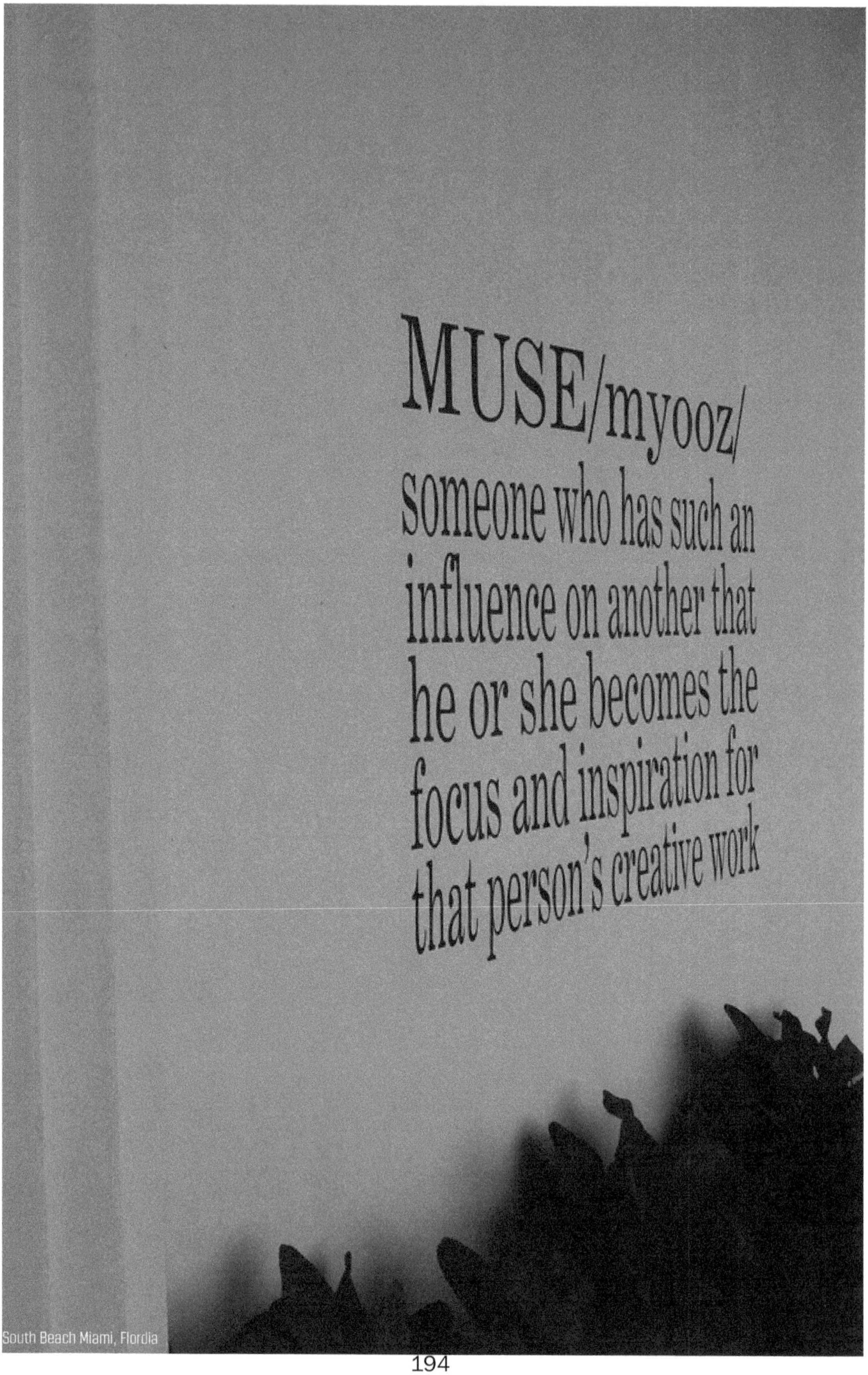
MUSE/myooz/
someone who has such an
influence on another that
he or she becomes the
focus and inspiration for
that person's creative work
South Beach Miami, Flordia

San Francisco, California.

Rose Quartz

meta+physical properties!

San Francisco, California.

sco, California

San Francisco, California.

San Francisco, California.

San Francisco, California.

San Francisco, California

THE POWER OF INTENTION

Everything in the universe has energy in it... everything has a vibration. It is a power that fulfills our desires and turns them into reality, it all starts with intention. We all have the power to manifest what we want in our lives. But first you must nurture body, mind, soul and spirit.

body: you are what you eat. treat your body as a temple and fill it with fresh foods. First you need to detox cleanse. thereafter find what foods that work for you, food allergies are actually quite common. Visit a Naturophathic Doctor, as I have found them to work more in depth when it comes to food allergies using non-toxic natural therapies, empathetic and overall phenomenal. With this said have the doctor create the proper regime for your body for optimal health and wellbeing. The doctor will make a lists of foods, suppliments that work best for your body and lifestyle. Remember try to eat fruits and vegtables that are organic.

mind: the mind is powerful but like a muscle we must keep it fit and healthy. Be present. Be mindful. meditate to vibrate positive vibes. keep your mind stimulated with brain teasers and games. read books, if you haven't a hobby find one that interests you, knitting, cooking, a cooking class, a musical instrument something that interests you, satisyfing.

spirit: is your life force energy. feed the spirit for strength to empower. vibrate high, through meditation and prayer, concentration on positive energy Dance.
Self-love. reverence for life. Self-care. Supportiveness. Live life in the present. Self-compassion. compassion. be present. mindful awareness. to receive love. to give love of family and community. in your diet eat high energy foods, superfoods; for natural beauty, anti-aging and longevity. living, plant foods; fruits, fermented foods. seeds, sprouts, grasses, and as they are living and have high vibrations that is beneficial for your lifeforce.

Soul: prayer. recite mantra's. chant the divine name. be love. **honor the Divine Feminine. Surrender to love for G_d/ Creator/Source. is LOVE.**

special note: in social media their are alot of opinions, pseudo-intellectuals that are not validated by truth. Please choose an authentic qualified Naturopathic Doctor.

SET YOUR INTENTIONS

write your intentions, this creates clarity to manifesting....

As much as you take from the universe and what the universe gives you, you must give back to receive, you just don't keep taking without giving" I have been told this throughout my theology teachings and studies countless times from sages, kabbalists, buddhists, hare krishnas, hinduism, Ifa priests, sufism, native american shaman and more... this messsage is universal.

Chapter 9

Pretty

Random

SEPTEMBER

YOU FIND YOURSELF WHEN YOU ARE CONSCIOUS & CLEANSED.

TAPPING INTO GODDESS ENERGY, THE GREAT MOTHER WHO LIVES AND RULES THE SEAS, YEMAYA. Take a trip to the beaCh.

Daytime or under the moonlight.

1. be present. light a blue Candle. light inCense in the sand.
2. meditate with Candle and inCense.
3. bathe naked if you Can, Cleansing in sea water.
4. slather molasses onto skin beautifully
5. ask for blessings & petition. meditate. wash off the molasses with the sea water.
6. swiping in a downward motion pass 7 white daisy's... flowers over your body starting with head to to feet, meditate on your desires. take the flowers in hand, give it to the ocean to Carry away the negativity and stress that you have been Carrying with your being.
7. offerings: bring seven different fruit and give them to her. (sample ideas; banana, apple, orange, pear, peach, mango or and watermelon is her favorite! Cover fruit with molasses and give to her. ebbo/offering in sand or when giving to oCean make sure it is organiC without pesticides. Leave 7 pennies or the equivalent of seven as this is Yemaya's number representative of the seven seas that belong to her, Yemaya is a Goddess who is motherly and strongly proteCtive, she also puts your life in order when you need it! Dress white or white and blue and wear for the rest of the day and sleep in white.

Wash off the following morning. Your going to feel TOTALLY AWESOME!

I AM

LIFE IS NOT COHESIVE

IT'S PRETTY RANDOM.

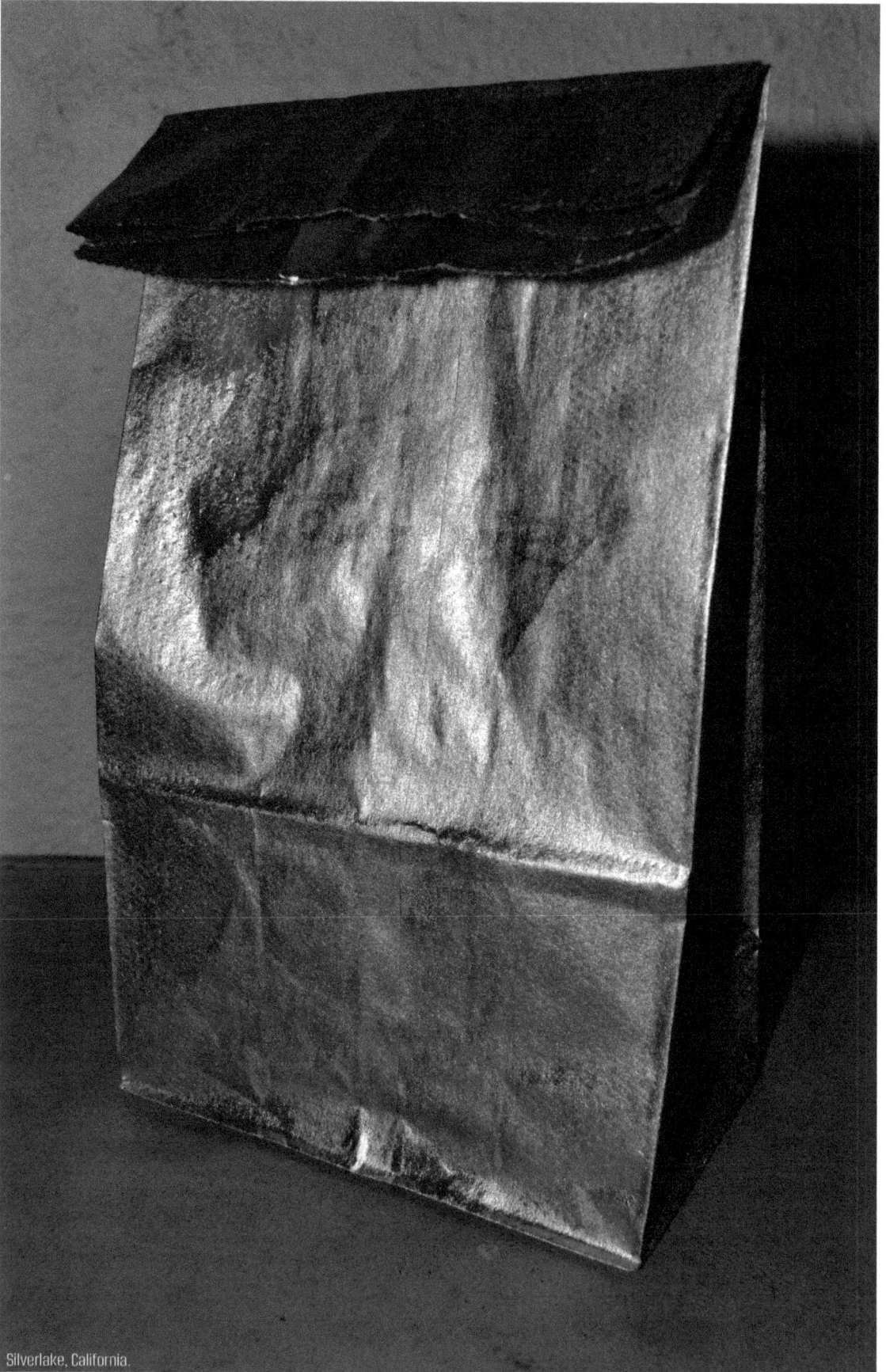

Silverlake, California.

"A Snowboarding Tradition" Park City, Utah.

Chapter 10

Celestial Juice

OCTOBER

...Compassion

Trick or treat? Every drop of water has a ripple effect, spreading kindness and love is the same thing, let love ripple and spread.

LOVE yourself, self+compassion WITH YOUR WHOLE HEART BODY, Mind AND SOUL. Love humankind, let this month be the beginning of spreading love, do something selfless and make it into becoming a daily thing by giving treats of smiles, good vibes and Love UNTO OTHERS, make it a daily lovefest of compassion.

meditate.... as to where you need to give love+compassion to feel no guilt.
there must be a balance of give and take in life for harmony.
what areas do you need to work on?

"Trick or treat."

OCTOBER!

totally Bitchen!

1. ROAD TRIP
2. Stay up for 24 hrs
3. wear red lipstick for breakfast whilst wearing a seethru white t-shirt white heels with your BFF at an outsid cafe. Have ur friend match. UNDERGARMDH: RED
4. Be positive
5. SKINNY DIP AT KO HIGH
6. MAKE MUDD PIES • MUDD WRESTLING > BACKYARD in ★ Bikini
7. HAVE A #3 NIGHT BLIND DATE MARDIS
8. Make love on the sand @ the beach in a bikini bloom.
9. Have a totally Bitchen day!
10. DRINK VODKA w/ fresh Pomegranate juice

DONT HAVE A BUCKET LIST, JUST LIVE

MAKE EVERYDAY COUNT

Gateway Arch. St. Louis, Missouri.

Downtown St. Louis, Missouri

221

Downtown Dallas, Texas.

Self+LOVE Rituals: for beauty
Moon water an ancient and sacred practice.
Super charged CRYSTAL INFUSED WATER
connect with the moon energy of the divine feminine power.
water is programmable.
Ingredients and directions
use Rose Quartz crystal(s):for self+love, beauty and attraction.
Get a clear glass, fill with water
Set your intention, speak into the water and Instill good vibes.
Put glass vessel/container and cover it. Place under the first full moon outside
or under a window sill, so it can gather the light of the moon. Indoors i also
lovingly light a blue or white candle beside the vessel. i also add a fresh
pressed rose elixir (or you can add 7 drops of rose water) as an added
vibration. Be creative in what you want to surround it with as i can get pretty
elaborate with the directions but this is a basic and simple yet supercharged
ritual. The following morning collect the vessel of the Moon Water, and give
thanks to the moon goddess of your liking.
this moon water is for drinking, spiritual baths and cleansing your spaces.
be mindful of what areas in your life where you need this magical water and
always be thoughtful and have gratitude, from the source that you are
tapping into. Love and Light.

note: not all crystals are safe to use. clean stones before usage.

you are your greatest
soulmate.
Love your+self daily
inside & out.

Before a night out

smudge

you're+self to

feel

confidence

for self+LOVE beauty &

attraction

KANSAS

Poconos, Pennsylvania.

Poconos, Pennsylvania

Santa Rosa, New Mexico.

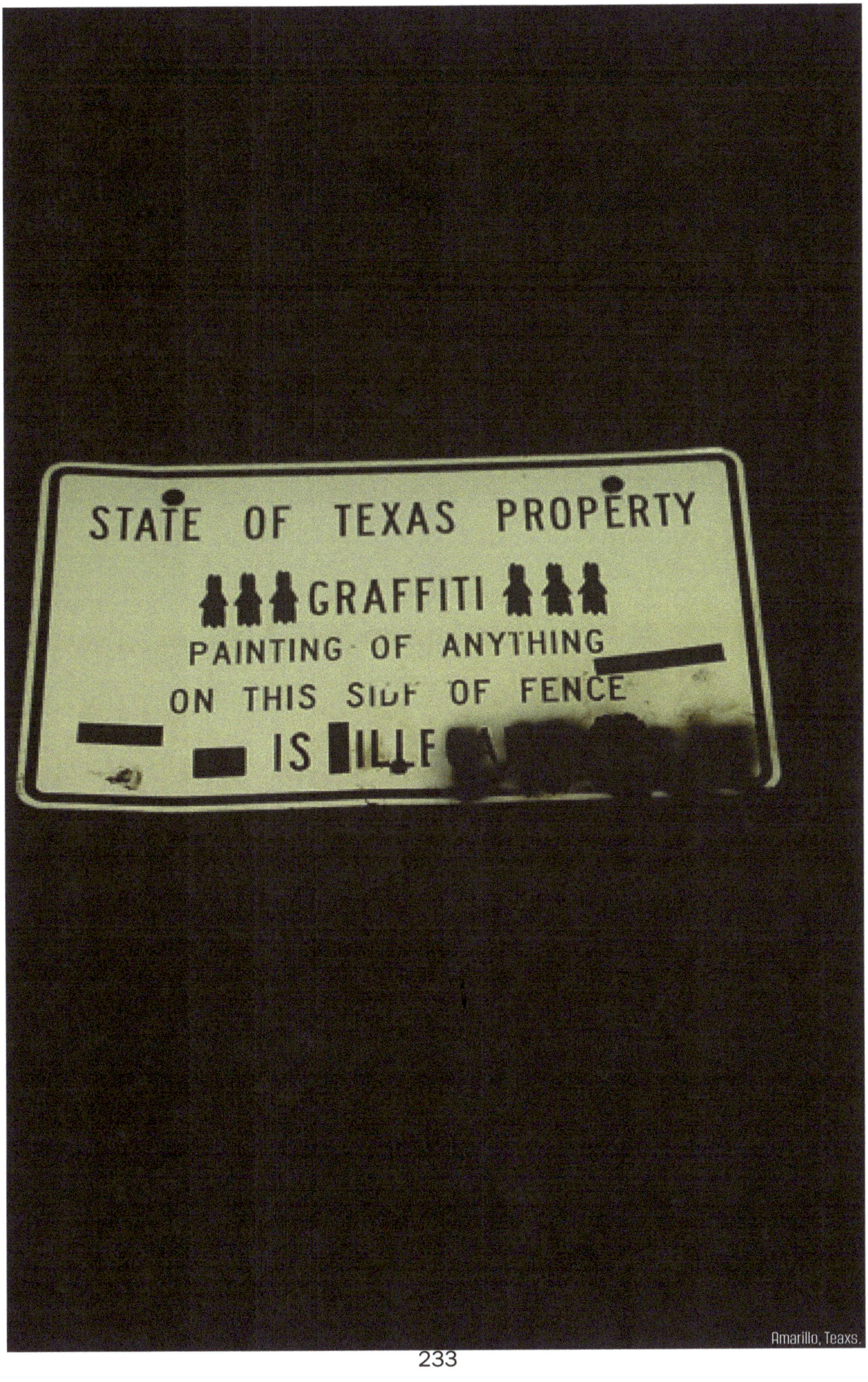

Amarillo, Teaxs.

Joplin, Missouri.

Chicago, Illinois.

Chapter 11

Hybrid Meditation

We / see What / we / want

NOVEMBER

Be forgiving. FORGIVE yourself, PRAY. meditate and LOVE.

I LOVE((YOU))
SAY I LOVE YOU OUT LOUD.
LOVE SOMEONE
UNCONDITIONALLY.
BE UNCONDITIONAL IN YOUR
FRIENDSHIPS & LOVE.

"UNCONDITIONAL LOVE."

Henderson Swamp, Louisiana.

Henderson Swamp, Louisiana.

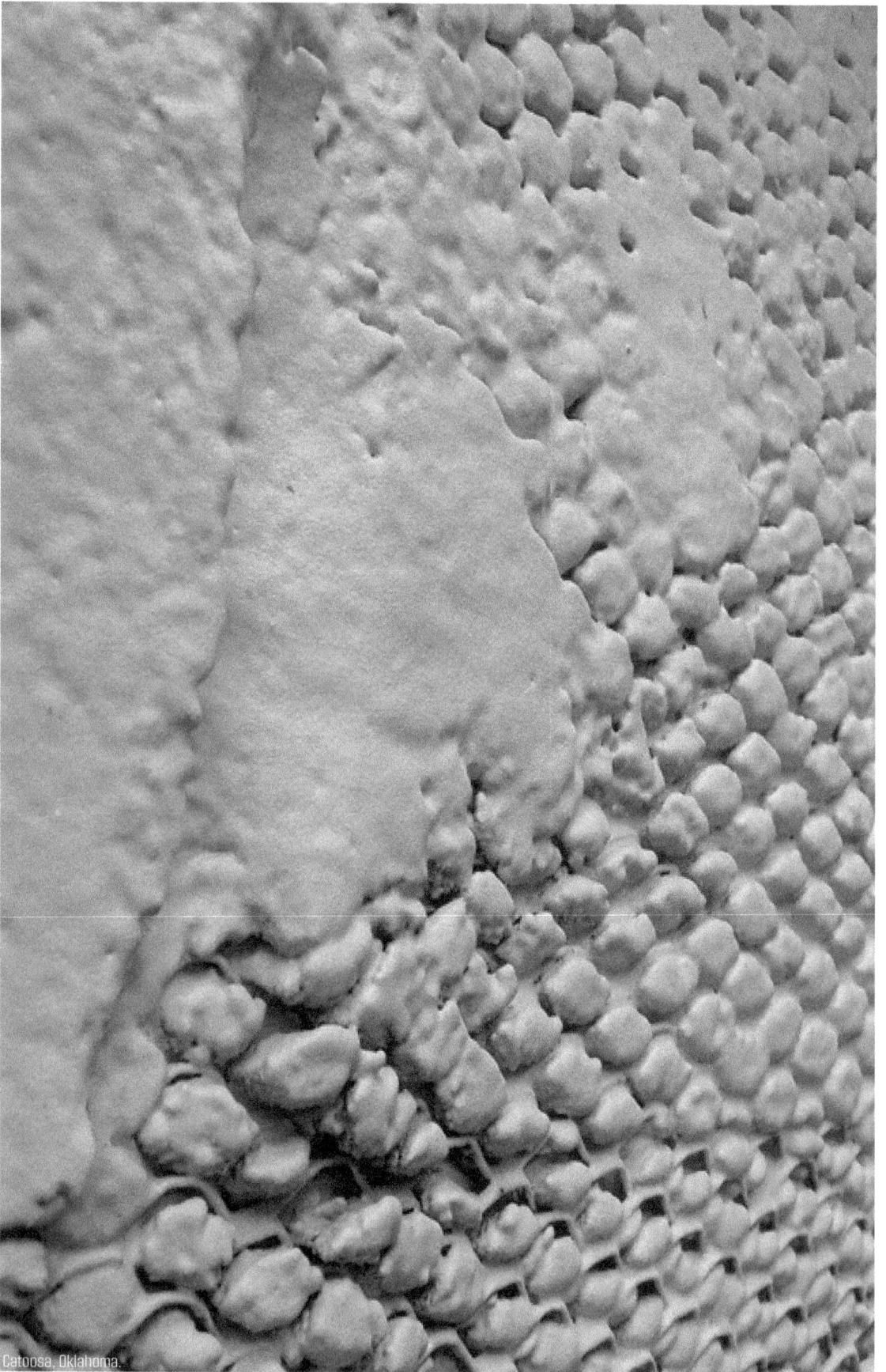

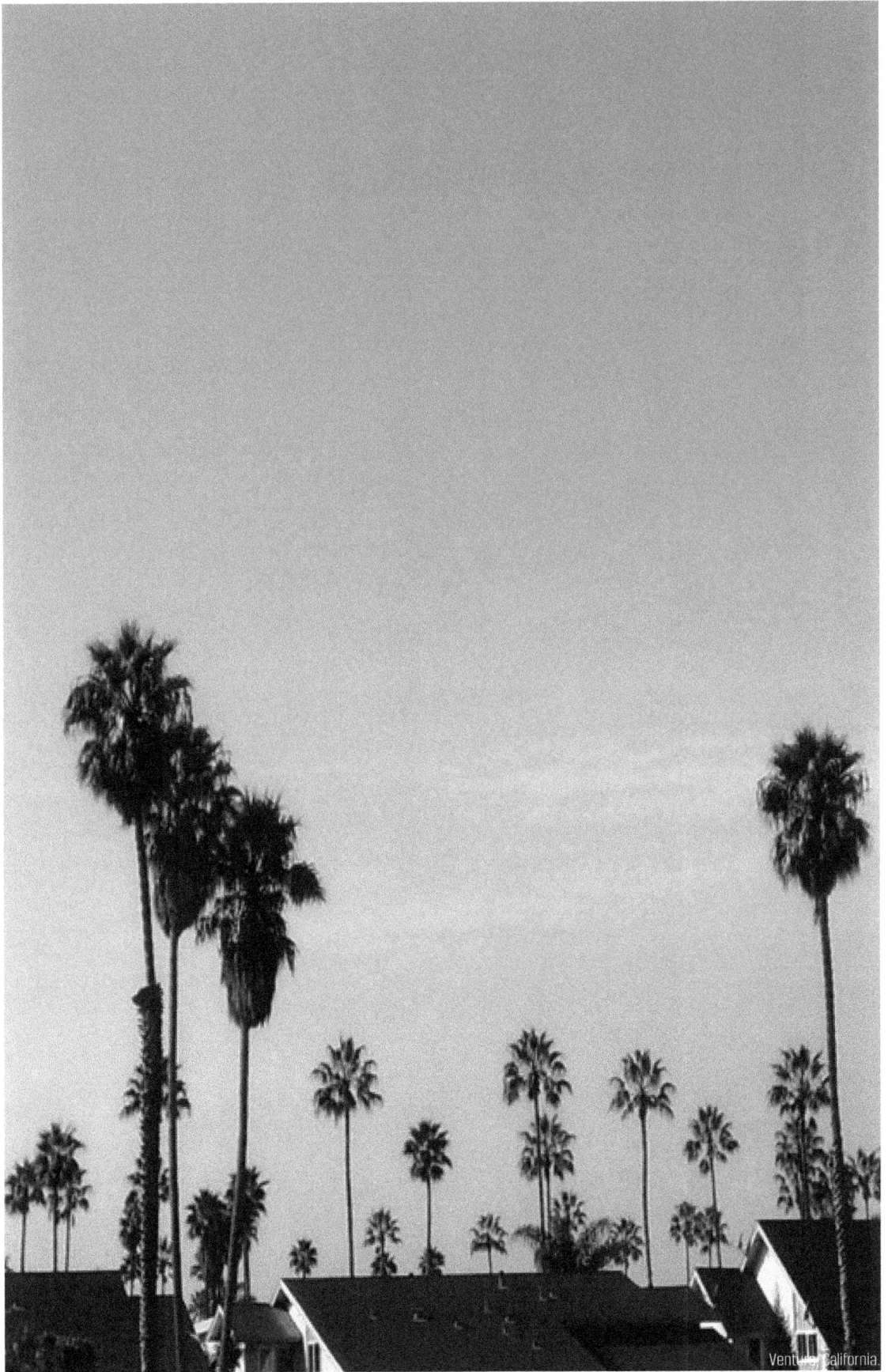

Ventura, California.

Chapter 12

HAPPY ENDINGS.

DECEMBER

Write on me!

"Write Without Restrictions"

San Luis Obispo, California.

San Luis Obispo, California

Upper East Side, New York.

Upper EaSt Side, New York.

Joseph City, Arizona.

MISSING BUNNY
HAVE YOU SEEN HIM

#FOLLOWTHEBUNNY

Palm Beach, Florida.

i LOVE YOU!
Hello Couture: Fetish Garden is a beautiful magical journey, it is an entire mind, body, and soul experience.

You are your authentic and greatest true love, soulmate. you are the writer in your own true story, life. You are deserving, all that is good and love.

Manifest...LIVE YOUR DREAMS AND MAKE THEM INTO REALITY
Open your eyes to profuse true beauty and pursue natures majestic corners, find yourself enthralled, harness the power you have from within surrounding yourself in beauty, you are tapping into the positive light love energy and it will help to guide you. All things are possible. Beauty is everywhere! Explore the open country, make time to enjoy life and you will see the beauty in the the most simplist of things. Remind yourself everyday, YES YOU can!

Daily, nourish your own fetish garden, be kind to yourself, treat yourself as the beautiful babe that you are, be love. Love everyone unconditionally, to make your world a fetish garden of peace, beauty and Love. No one is perfect, yet try your best to always take the high road and see things in a positive way. Be a vessel of love and light for other's and yourself.

Goddess mindset, is loving yourself. i am a messenger here to share ancestral tools of enlightment.
Calm your mind, visualize your desires while connecting to your energy, relax. Come to the realization that you are a spiritual being. i want you to love yourself and live your best life. You are worthy of love, you are manifested from love. Detox yourself of self-loathing , i want you to love yourself and live your best life. Rise into your authentic power. Claim your empowerment today. Awaken self+love. You are the creator. You are what you think, focus only on the positive. With self-love you can manifest your desires. Set intentions. I want you to say everyday that, i am... i exist. Find your true pleasure in life and do it! Get a daily journal, write only positive words from your day, focus only on the positive and be aware of how your changing and growing for the better. The path to happiness is quite simple, leave past baggage behind, live in the present and find pleasure in loving yourself. You have the tools to find the Guru within. Meditate daily.

This journey could not be summarized in one book, this work is a continuing process, like life. My wish I make is that you find your divinity, this book is going to help you. Until we meet again....peace, Love & Light. #lubovlovetribe
LOVE always, Priestess/Shaman Lubov

South Beach Miami, Florida

"THE Self-LOVE Party
STARTS NOW."

"LIFE IS NOT COHESIVE AND IN THAT REGARD
NEITHER SHOULD ART. LIFE IS PRETTY RANDOM."
Channah Morozuykova

South Beach Miami, Florida.